THE PHILOSOPHY OF JESUS

. . . for the World Today

THE PHILOSOPHY OF JESUS

... for the World Today

ERNEST HOLMES

Compiled and Edited by
WILLIS KINNEAR

SCIENCE OF MIND COMMUNICATIONS
LOS ANGELES, CALIFORNIA

Seventh Printing — August 1991

Science of Mind Communications wishes to acknowledge
Mrs. Marion Warfield Hefferlin
through whose generosity this seventh printing was made possible.

Published by Science of Mind Communications

CONTENTS

FOREWORD

For far too long the basic philosophy and teaching of Jesus has been shrouded in archaic terminology and as a result it does not fit into today's world. The fundamental spiritual truths he advanced do have practical meaning for us today if properly understood.

For many years the late Ernest Holmes, one of the great religious philosophers of our day, spoke of the meaning and significance of the work of Jesus. In this connection he taught others how they could start doing the "greater works" Jesus said they should do.

The material in this volume has been selected from Dr. Holmes' unpublished manuscripts and arranged in a sequence that will enable the reader to gain a fuller comprehension of the impact that the philosophy of Jesus can have on the world today.

In many respects the ideas may be startling, but on the other hand they have proved to be of great value in the lives of people who have used them.

Great truths are timeless, but cultures and patterns of thinking change. What has been done in these pages is an attempt to more fully understand the message of Jesus as it relates to your life today.

I

THE POWER THAT JESUS USED

Throughout our lives we have read and wondered about the miracles of Jesus. But to how many of us has the thought come that this same power must be available to everyone? We have been so accustomed to thinking of Jesus as a man filled with love and compassion and human kindness that we have overlooked something else about him that is equally important. Jesus had access to a spiritual Power that he used in every way. To him it seemed the most natural thing in the world that he should be able to tell the paralyzed man to walk, or multiply the loaves and fishes, or still the wind and waves.

I happen to be one of those who really believe that Jesus did these things and that we could also do them if we had the know-how. It takes nothing away from Jesus when we say that in addition to his love and compassion and his great humanity we also have access to the same Power which enabled him to do such wonderful things. Even his own followers thought he must be using a power that no one else possessed; however, when we study his words carefully, we find that he said that others could do what he did if they followed the same rules. Jesus was not the great exception, he was the great example, and he even said that "greater works than these shall he do; because I go unto my Father."

What we want to find out, then, is the nature of this Power that Jesus used, learn how It operates, and then apply It in our own lives in helping ourselves and also in helping others. I am not thinking only about the healing miracles when people have been restored to physical health. For while this is wonderful and good, there is much more to life than merely getting rid of a pain. Jesus had access to some kind of Power that was available for every purpose. He had access to an Intelligence that guided him in everything he did. And he had a deep inward peace and feeling of security that removed all confusion and doubt and uncertainty from his mind.

What we want to find is the key that unlocks the doorway to the Power greater than we are. What we want to do is to discover the secret which he so plainly told us was a certain kind of relationship he had to God, who, he said, was present everywhere and was also within him and within everyone.

We are accustomed to thinking of the powers and energies in nature, and we know that the whole field of modern science is devoted to the discovery of these powers and learning how to apply them for our everyday needs. We also know that these powers which science uncovers have always existed, they were always there waiting to be used, always ready to respond when we use them rightly.

We think of a scientific man as one who uses a power of nature. We do not say that he possesses it as a personal thing. For, of course, this would not be true. What we say is that science discovers the power, unlocks its energy, and then uses it for definite purposes for the betterment of humanity. What we really mean by this is that there are certain physical laws and physical powers in nature which are greater than we are but which can be used, and that these powers operate for us as though they were our servants. We employ them, we do not implore them. That is, we do not beseech them, we do not coerce them, and, as a matter of fact, we do not even concentrate them. We merely use them.

But Jesus had access to another kind of power which he called the Power of the Spirit. We cannot doubt but that there are spiritual powers which act like physical ones; that act for us and in a certain sense become our servants when we have first learned how they operate. But in doing this we must always comply with them, for the secrets of nature are disclosed and the powers of nature can be used only when we first comply with the way they work. Of all people in the world the true scientist is the most humble. He stands in reverence and awe before the wonders of a self-operating universe that operates independently of his will, his coercion, or even his desire.

When it was discovered that a hen lays a certain number of eggs and then sits on them and hatches out chickens, someone had the foresight to realize that you can have as many hens as you want to sit on as many eggs as they can cover and produce as many chickens as are desirable, provided you actually put the hen and the eggs together. Here is an example of the way nature works, with complete independence of our thoughts and our will and our desires, but always with this in mind, that when we comply with the way she works, we receive the benefit.

And so it is with every scientific discovery. In the laboratory man observes the laws of nature, discovers how they work, and then applies them, and nature herself produces the result. We are so used to thinking of this that we take it for granted, not realizing that every day, in some physical laboratory, new things are being revealed to us because we are learning how to cooperate with the Source of all power.

Jesus worked in a different kind of laboratory. He understood a different set of laws, and because he used these laws a power was delivered to him that has amazed the world. It is our purpose to rediscover these laws, find out how they work, and apply them for every legitimate purpose, then reap the benefit for ourselves and for others. Of course, in doing this it is necessary that we follow the example of the one who really knew. The only reason we have to suppose that Jesus knew is that he proved his claim. What we should do, then, is to find out exactly what Jesus believed, and why, and how he used this secret of the ages so effectively.

The first thing we shall learn is that Jesus believed himself to be one with God, and he believed that the Divine Presence was right where he was. He communed with this Presence through prayer and meditation until It was the most real thing to him in life. But Jesus added something else to this, for he told us that after we have discovered God and when we have learned to commune with Him through prayer and meditation, then a certain kind of spiritual Power will be delivered to us, if we have faith that It will. We find, then, that the whole background of his teaching starts with the idea that there is such a Presence and such a Power; that the Presence is accessible to all of us, and that the Power can be used by anyone who has faith in It.

This is no doubt the greatest secret of the ages. It is the miracle of the answer to prayer. It is the miracle of Life Itself. We need to believe that you and I, so little and so alone, do have access to a Power that has the possibility of making everything in our lives happy and harmonious if we cooperate with It. Right here I would like to inject this thought — for it is one that so many people express — how can we believe in a Power that we can neither touch nor taste nor handle?

The answer to this is simple enough. Let us go right back to the hen sitting on her eggs. Neither you nor I nor the hen ever put a chicken in an egg, nor did we ever take one out. The hen, instinctively, by some method of which she is not consciously aware, follows the law of her own life. She lays the eggs and then she sits on them and nature performs the miracle for her. The Power which does this cannot be touched or tasted or handled. It cannot be seen. And yet, we are so used to it that we never question the result. We build incubators and set the eggs in them and subject them to a certain heat for a certain period of time, with complete assurance, with absolute faith, because experience has taught us that we can do this and have chicks hatch.

So it is with every law that we use. No one has ever seen the powers of nature. We only see how they work and we accept them with the simplicity of a child. Again someone might ask: How can we believe in a Divine Presence when we have not seen It? The answer to this also is simple. How can we believe in the law of attraction and repulsion which we have not seen? How can we believe that a magnet will attract iron since we do not see the power of attraction that draws it? No one has ever seen love or human affection, no one has seen kindness and tolerance and human understanding, but we have all felt them and we have no more doubt of their existence than we do of our own being.

I do not think we need to be concerned with the fact that we do not see God other than in His creation, or that we have not seen the forces of nature other than in and through what they do. When Jesus told us that we should have faith, he was not telling us about something that is impossible for us to attain, for Jesus was the most simple and direct of men and he knew that faith is a natural attitude of mind. It is the very simplicity of his teaching that eludes us. As a matter of fact, it is so easy that it is hard, so simple that it is difficult, so direct that we fail to catch its significance. For whether or not we know it, we all have faith. We are merely mostly using it in reverse.

So Jesus told us that there is a Divine Presence that will guide us if we let It. And he told us that there is a Power that will operate for us if we believe that It will. But he also told us that this Presence is love and this Power is good and that we cannot hope to derive the greatest benefit from the Presence as Divine guidance, or the Power as the operation of Divine Love, until we first greet the Presence in love and use the Power for good. So far as I know, he laid down no instructions other than these: God is love and God is good, therefore Divine Power is delivered to us only in such degree as we love and as we are constructive.

All the prayers or the will of man can neither add to nor take from the powers of nature. This is so self-evident that one cannot even argue against it. What we have to do, then, is to invite the Presence and use the Power. We invite the Divine Presence every time we think about It in love and with true humility. We draw inspiration into our minds and into our imaginations and loose it through our actions when we recognize this Presence, and we benefit from the use of the Power when we comply with the way It works.

Here is where our great experiment in using the Power that Jesus understood starts. This is the very beginning of it. We must believe that there is a Divine Presence. Of course, our belief does not create It; it merely acknowledges It. It is this acknowledgment of the Divine Presence that Jesus was referring to when he said: " . . . your Father knoweth what things ye have need of, before ye ask him."

The artist believes in the presence of beauty. He invites it into his thought and will and imagination; he makes himself open to it. Our acknowledgment of the Presence of God should be as simple as this and as direct. No matter what we are doing we should start with this basic thought: "God is all there is. God is right where I am. Divine Intelligence is now directing me. I not only invite It, I believe It is here. There is nothing in me that can deny me the privilege of receiving this Divine guidance. There is Something in me that knows what to do under every circumstance, knows how to meet every situation, knows how to overcome every obstacle. I am in partnership with the infinite Mind that creates everything and sustains everything. I am one with God."

We should entertain thoughts like these until they become habitual; that is, until nothing in us denies them. It is not going to take any more faith than we now have, for one of the greatest lessons we can learn about faith is that we always possess it. But too often we are using it negatively. As a matter of fact, we are always affirming something, be it for good or for ill. We are always either saying, "I can," or "I cannot." What we need to do is to eliminate the negative and accentuate the positive. In doing this we shall gradually acquire the habit of affirmative thinking.

To this belief that there is a Divine Presence which is guiding us and leading us gently but certainly on the pathway to success and happiness and wholeness, we must also come to believe that there is a Power that always goes with this recognition of the Divine Presence, and we must have faith that this Power operates on our word. But, of course, we do not see Its operation. We do not touch It or taste It or handle It, but we can feel It. It is this deep underlying conviction and feeling that we must acquire.

But this is not difficult. It is just a question of training the mind to believe in and understand spiritual Law in exactly the same manner that it believes in and understands the operation of physical law. If it were something too difficult, then it would be beyond our reach and we should become discouraged even before we started. The whole thing has to be kept simple and direct and sincere. The Power that Jesus used was a spiritual Power. He knew that It operated on or through his word of faith, and he had such complete reliance on It that he did not hesitate to tell the paralyzed man to get up and walk.

It was not the words that Jesus used that performed the miracle. It was his inner conviction of the Power that operated on and in and through his words. He called this faith and belief, and in so doing reduced it to a mental attitude or to a way of thinking that we all can understand. There is Something that operates on our belief and acts exactly like a law, because It is a law, and tends to bring about conditions which correspond to our faith, our belief, our way of thinking.

Frequently, when we begin to use this Power consciously we find that our thoughts are unruly. In one moment we affirm some good we desire and in the very next moment we deny what we have affirmed. In this way we are a mental house divided against itself. We may as well recognize this fact because it is an important one. But in recognizing it there is no occasion for us to despair. For we know that thinking is really a movement of the mind upon itself, right where we are, and we are the thinker, therefore we can change our thoughts.

This is why Jesus told us that sometimes only prayer and fasting can bring about the desired result. He did not mean that God listens because we do a lot of talking. What he meant was that we should pray affirmatively and fast when it comes to negative thinking. This is the sacrifice we make in the surrender of our doubts and fears to the great affirmations of life. To pray without ceasing means to continue in an affirmative attitude of mind and to fast means to refrain from all negative thoughts and ideas.

There must come a new impulse to the mind, a new way of looking at things. This is what Jesus called the new birth. He referred to this when he said that we must be born again, we must be born of the Spirit, which means being born into a complete conviction of the Presence and the Power and the Activity of God in and through us. The results that follow this new birth are automatic, and this is why Jesus told us that if we would seek the kingdom of God first, everything else would be added.

What a wonderful adventure lies before us. How grateful we should be for the opportunity to live and love and work and play. We should have a keen sense of anticipation and enthusiasm because we know that we are working with a spiritual Power greater than we are, a Law of Mind that is available to create every good thing in life. I believe this is the secret to the power Jesus demonstrated and to the understanding of his teachings. We may call this faith, we may call it religion, we may call it worship. It is all this and more, too. But in reality it resolves itself into a simple, sincere, and direct approach to God and to the Law of Mind.

The world is in search of the answer to its problems. Frustrated and distraught, disillusioned and chagrined, today it stands on the brink of two possibilities — to be, or not to be. The world today is shocked by the realization of what it has brought on itself. Nothing is more certain than that we have failed, and as never before millions of people are ready to try something else, that something that for too long has been neglected, that something which alone can make it whole. Nothing is more certain than that we must rediscover the secret of the ages, this coming into close cooperation with the Presence that made us and the Power that sustains us. Along this pathway alone lies the hope of humanity. This, and this only, is the road to peace, to prosperity, and to happiness.

II

ONE MAN WITH GOD

In all the years that I have worked intimately with so many people I have never yet found one individual who did not secretly long to find something that would make him whole and happy, something that would give him a sense of security and safety. I have never yet found an individual who did not wish the same good for others. I am a great believer in the innate goodness of people, and I know, through much experience, that the average person wants to do about the best he can.

Frequently when I have said to people, "Why don't you learn to use spiritual Power so that It will be effective in your life and in the lives of those around you?" the answer has been: "But I don't know how," or, "I haven't the faith," or, "I haven't the training or the education," or, "I haven't the opportunity."

I guess this is the sort of alibi we all use because it does not occur to us that we have to start right where we are, and, using such faith as we possess, acquire more through actual experience.

Jesus definitely set about to prove what one man with God could do. He demonstrated for all ages that just one person, with implicit faith, can do anything. If there is any one fact that Jesus emphasized beyond all others it was that what he was doing others could do also, if they believed they could and if they believed in God.

Jesus knew that one man with God is a majority. As we look back over his life and rethink its meaning, we discover that he had trained himself to believe in God. To him the Presence of God was as real as sunshine, as definite as the wind blowing. So great was his concept of the Power of God that he said that heaven and earth would pass away but his words would not until all be fulfilled.

This, then, is the kind of faith we are called on to have. But it is not a faith that is found in books. It is not a faith that someone else can give to us, because no one can possibly give us that which we already possess. Rather, it is something we now have but have not been using and we have not been using it because we have not recognized that it is already right where we are.

One man with God is a wonderful idea, and it will be even more wonderful when we realize that that one man is ourself. But that one man is not ourself unless we include God. It is one man *with* God that we must emphasize. God exists everywhere and in Him we live and move and have our being. The Spirit is within us as well as around us and we can have no life apart from It. All the life of the Spirit, then, belongs to each one of us, but, in a certain sense, we only have as much as we use.

Again, as we reflect on the life and teaching of Jesus, we find that he spent much time alone, communing with God. In his instructions he tells us that the Power of God acts independently of any circumstance because It creates circumstances. When we get lost in the circumstances that surround us and become confused over them, and when we feel isolated and alone, then it is that the struggle for existence becomes unbearable and we feel that the odds are against us. This is why Jesus told us not to judge according to the appearance, but to judge righteously, that is, we should not look at the obstruction in our lives and say it is too great to overcome. We should know that even in the obstruction which confronts us, at the very center of it, there is a Power that can resolve all obstacles, solve all problems, and meet every emergency.

So it becomes a question of whether our faith is greater than the obstruction; whether we are becoming confused over conditions or thinking peacefully and calmly about them. When it comes right down to a rock-bottom fact, the only question is whether or not we believe in a Power greater than we are that we can use, and whether or not we actually believe that this Power is ready, willing, and able to respond to us.

Let us turn back to the instruction of the one who knew what he was talking about when he said: ". . . it is your Father's good pleasure to give you the kingdom." Life has made the gift but we must accept it. We cannot doubt that there must have been, particularly in the beginning of his ministry, doubts that arose in his mind just as they do in ours. We can visualize Jesus standing in the midst of a multitude who were clamoring for healing, bringing their sick and lame and blind to him, and as he looked out over this vast sea of faces, perhaps the question came to him: Can I make these people whole?

But we know what his answer was, for he said: "I can of mine own self do nothing . . . but the Father that dwelleth in me, he doeth the works." We can almost sense that triumphant concept that arose in his consciousness — the realization that one man with God is supreme; that he, as a human being, had no power of himself at all, but that all power was given to him in heaven and on earth because he had acquired all love and because he had become intimate with that Divine Presence which flows through everything.

The power that Jesus manifested was Divine. It was not the will of an individual, but his willingness to believe that gave him power. It was not a concentration of spiritual forces that Jesus exercised, but rather, a childlike and implicit faith in the reality of the Spirit in human affairs.

One of the most amazing things about this man was that he never tried to influence anyone. He was not at all like the alleged psychological individual who had developed such a terrific personality that his influence dominated others. This is exactly what Jesus did not do and warned us against trying to do. Quite the reverse from this, Jesus said that the kingdom of God is like a child. It is simplicity and sincerity. It is quiet acceptance rather than loud proclamation.

Keeping this in mind let us think of Jesus feeding the multitude. His disciples had asked him to disperse the crowd that they might go home where there would be food for them. But Jesus turned to his disciples and asked why they did not feed the multitude. And they replied that they had nothing with which to feed them. "There is a lad here, which hath five barley loaves, and two small fishes: but what are they among so many?"

Perhaps here is one of the greatest lessons in spiritual history. Jesus must have been surrounded by people of great knowledge. There were the doctors of law who thought they knew all the answers, trying to catch him in a trap. There were his own followers, who, although they had seen many miracles, could not believe that Jesus was able to feed the multitude out of nothing. And there was the young boy with a few loaves and fishes, standing eager and expectant and holding out his meager fare to the hands of Jesus, who took the loaves and fishes, gave thanks and broke them, and distributed them to the multitude.

Let us think of this not only as an actual reality — which I most sincerely believe — but as a symbol of ourselves. For there is a little boy in each one of us. There is a hope and an inward spiritual realization in everyone, something that is beyond all doubt, fear, and uncertainty. We would not be here if this were not true.

Let us think of this beautiful symbol — the intellect and the human will surrendering itself to some inward feeling, some childlike simplicity, some spontaneous joy, some complete faith. Yes, that child is in you and in me and experience has never completely dimmed its vision. It is that within us which is childlike that we must cultivate. For the child within us knows a language that the intellect has failed to learn.

Let us think of Jesus standing before the tomb of Lazarus where the friends and relatives had gathered, hoping at least to find some comfort from his words, but not even daring to dream that Lazarus could be resurrected from the dead. Jesus stood there in front of the tomb — one man alone with God. He stood just a little apart from the others and lifted up his soul in silent communion with the Spirit of all life, that Spirit that knows no death. Something flowed into him and he turned around and said: "Take ye away the stone." But they remonstrated that Lazarus had been dead for four days and they dare not roll away the stone.

Now let us watch carefully what Jesus did and listen to his words as he said: "Father, I thank thee that thou hast heard me. And I knew that thou hearest me always. . . . " This is recognition of the Divine Presence and the Divine Power that is always available. Here is faith and unification. There was no doubt, no uncertainty, no stammering or stuttering, no imploring or beseeching. Just the simple words: "I thank thee" (gratitude) "that thou hearest me always" (certainty).

Next comes the supreme command: "Lazarus, come forth." One man with God, recognizing life instead of death until the tomb surrendered its dead and Lazarus came forth and Jesus told them to "loose him, and let him go."

Lazarus is each one of us, bound by the restriction of circumstances, tied by the habits of thought, and incarcerated in a tomb from which it seems as though we cannot extricate ourselves. "Loose him, and let him go." There is much in each one of us that must be loosed — the ropes of fear that bind us, the winding sheet of doubt and uncertainty, the darkness and gloom of our self-imposed prison, and the stone that must be rolled away. Yes, and the doubt of others who would block the action of faith because all they see is the stone and the tomb and the dead man inside; and they say: "You dare not roll away the stone."

Let us think of the silent communion we have with the Spirit that knows no bondage, with the Life that knows no death, and with the Power that knows no obstruction. As we do this something within us comes alive and awake and aware and gives us the courage and the assurance to say, "Father, I thank thee that thou hast heard me, and I knew that thou hearest me always." Out of this communion comes a Divine authority which is the gift only of heaven.

One man with God — and you are that man and I am that man. Just one, for in that silent inward precinct of our own minds no one enters but ourselves. Something within us stands halfway between heaven and earth — the child who is not afraid and the man of wisdom who has overcome fear. There is one side of us that has never entered the shadow of doubt. This is what we must develop if we are to prove that one man with God can be supreme in whatever is right, just, or true — just one man with God.

III

THE SCIENCE OF PRAYER

One of the outstanding things about the teaching of Jesus was that he did not reserve the use of spiritual Power for some future event, but boldly proclaimed that the kingdom of God is here and now and that the Law of Mind is available for every legitimate and constructive human purpose. Jesus said that whatsoever things we desire, when we pray, we should believe that we have them. He said that unless our prayers are amiss, that is, unless they are contrary to good, they will be answered.

Jesus healed the sick, and yet one of his immediate followers was a physician. I think one of the things the world should be experimenting with today is exactly what Dr. Robert A. Millikan suggested: combining religion and faith and prayer with all the wonderful things now being worked out in the field of medicine. I believe that when we combine psychosomatic medicine, which is body-mind relationships, with spiritual Power, we will have gone a long way toward finding the road to health. Most physicians prefer to have a patient who has faith, and the more observing one prefers a household of faith surrounding his patient.

Jesus in many ways demonstrated the availability of the Law of Mind to meet human needs, wherever and whenever they arose. Perhaps we have fallen into the mistake of thinking that the Law is available only for a few purposes. We should use spiritual Power in everything we do, and we should have such a complete evidence that this Power actually exists that there will be no question about it in our minds. Jesus said that "these signs shall follow them that believe." Taking his teaching as the great example, we should expect signs following our prayers of faith.

The question then arises: If there is such a Power, why is it that all our prayers are not answered? A great many sincere people believe that God answers only certain prayers and not others. But another smaller group believes that all prayers will be answered when we pray aright.

It was this latter position that Jesus took. He very carefully explained what he meant by right prayer. Right prayer, according to his teaching, includes the good of the other fellow as well as ourselves. For instance, he said that we should love our neighbors as we love ourselves. But in saying this we should carefully note that Jesus did not say we must hate ourselves in order to love our neighbors. He knew that we are all important to God. We should love ourselves for what we really are, and we should love our neighbors for what they really are. We should wish to do good to others, and we should desire that good will be done unto us.

I believe that we pray aright when there is nothing in our prayers that would hurt anyone. I believe we pray aright when we pray unselfishly. This does not mean that we should exclude ourselves. It does mean that we should include others. Then surely our prayers will be in accord with Divine Love and Wisdom.

What can we do with the spiritual Power which is closer to us than our very breath? How shall we so attune ourselves to It that good will flow out in all directions and return to us a hundredfold? I think that first we must come to believe that there actually is such a Power and that we really can use It.

We believe that there is a law of gravitation which holds us in the position in which we place ourselves, and we have implicit faith in this law. We have faith in it and we are so accustomed to

the idea that we never question it. This is the first great require-
ment of the teaching of Jesus, that we must believe. Let us think
of spiritual Power, then, as a natural Law, and let us think of faith
and prayer as the right way to use this Law. For prayer is our
communion with the Spirit and faith is our definite acceptance
that through this communion the Law of Mind reacts to us and to
others according to our belief.

Here is where religion, faith, prayer, and science can combine.
For communion with the Divine Presence helps us to arrive at the
place of faith and acceptance, and it is this faith and this acceptance that make prayer powerful.

But it might be asked: Why can't you have the faith without
the communion? My answer would be another question: Can an
artist paint a beautiful picture unless he communes with beauty?
I believe that this is true when we seek to combine the prayer of
faith with communion with the Spirit. God is peace, God is love,
God is life, and God is beauty. When we become peaceful and
commune with this life and love and beauty, something happens
to us inside. It is as though a great power were flowing into us. And
so, if someone were to ask: Why can't we have faith without communion? my answer would be: It is communion that gives us
faith.

The next step is to make God real to our own mind. This is
something each has to work out for himself. God is love, therefore
we should open up our minds to love. God is peace, therefore we
should become receptive to peace. God is good, therefore we
should meditate on goodness. When we sit quietly by ourselves
and think of God as very close to us, and think of love and peace
and goodness as the great Reality, a surge of faith uplifts our
mind.

Now we are ready to pray effectively, which merely means we
are ready to make our spiritual affirmations with complete conviction because we know that we are dealing with a Power greater
than we are, a Power that we do not coerce or coax or intrigue,

because It is already here, It is right where we are. This Power apparently flows through our words and is a Divine Law which always tends to produce the good we have accepted.

We should train our minds to think affirmatively. This means that we must winnow out all negations. We must dispel the darkness of doubt and fear. We could not do this if we felt we were depending on our own personal power, any more than we believe we could use any other law in nature through exercising willpower or coercion.

When we use prayer affirmatively we get results. So we should train ourselves to expect definite results when we use spiritual Power. This is done through what is called meditation or affirmative prayer. We start with the thought that God is all there is: "There is one Life, that Life is God, that Life is my life now." If we are praying for physical well-being we might say: "There is one Life, that Life is God, that Life is my life now, that Life is animating every organ and every function of my physical being. It is circulating through me, filling me with perfect Life. All the energy and all the action and all the vitality that there is is pouring through me *now*."

If we wish to pray affirmatively for someone else, we would say: "This Life is flowing through him now." When we pray affirmatively for another we are recognizing God in him, we are thinking of God as being his life, his power, his strength, his vitality. We are definitely stating that this is the way it is.

If we will practice this, patiently and persistently, over a period of time, we will be amazed at the results. What a wonderful experiment this will be! It is perhaps the greatest adventure we will ever make. As we begin to see the signs following our spiritual communion and our affirmative belief, we will be given an assurance, a faith, and a conviction such as never came to us before.

We are already familiar with the idea of psychosomatic medicine, or body-mind relationships, but now we are adding to this spiritual-psychosomatic medicine, or using the power of the Spirit to so direct the mind that the mind will rightly control the body. This is the next step to be taken in the advance of the curative arts.

In doing this we do not deny the mind, nor the important place it must have in our everyday lives. But we do affirm something else — the presence of the Spirit, the realization of the Divine Presence in everything and through everyone, and the Power of the Law of Mind.

Gradually, as we reach out and begin to use this Power for definite purposes it will become as natural to begin to affirm the Divine Presence when we get up in the morning as it has been to wonder what is going to happen during the day. For we will feel that we are no longer alone, buffeted by fate; we have a Divine Companion, an infinite Intelligence, and an all-powerful Good cooperating with us.

IV

EFFECTIVE PRAYER

There is no doubt but that there is a Power for good in the universe which we can and should use. The question then is: Why don't we use It more effectively? If all things are possible to faith, why don't we have more faith? And if affirmative prayers are answered, why don't we always pray affirmatively?

It does seem a little strange, since we all want success and happiness, that we might be keeping them away from us without knowing it. One of the most interesting things we can consider is the working of our mind in its relationship with the Power greater than we are. Let us try to figure out just how the Law of Mind works and how we can better cooperate with It.

I would like to begin with the thought that we are all united with invisible forces which are creative; that we are already one with a universal Law of Mind which can do anything, and one with the Divine Intelligence which knows all things.

The next thing for us to consider is that we are thinking and active centers in this Mind, and that the sum total of all our thoughts is either silently attracting our good to us or repelling it from us.

The third proposition is that we can change our thinking, and, in so doing, cause the Law to act affirmatively for us instead of negatively.

Let us start with the first idea, that we are surrounded by a creative Law of Mind which reacts to our thought. This is the basis of all effective prayer, and this is why Jesus told us that when we pray we should believe we already have what we desire. He implied that there is a Power that can and will and must react to us. But he also implied that when this Power reacts to us It has no choice other than to react to us according to the way we think.

I do not think we have quite understood the significance and the full meaning of this bold claim that Jesus made. For no one else had ever said it in the same way before. Up until the time of Jesus those who preceded him had said that God might help us, that there were concessions He would make if we pleased Him, if we performed certain rites or ceremonials. This was good and helpful, but Jesus changed these suppositions into certainties. He said simply and directly that there is a Power that operates on our belief the way we believe. But he added that even the Law, which is all-powerful, can only bring us as much good as we accept. This accepting is an act of our own mind; it is an act of faith.

It has been only within the last hundred years or less that people have come to realize that Jesus was talking about a spiritual Principle in which we all are rooted, which operates on our faith, our conviction, and our acceptance. I have no doubt that within the next hundred years the world will fully accept this. But we cannot wait so long. What we should do is to come to understand exactly what Jesus was talking about and realize that he meant what he said.

It is the very simplicity of his claim that causes us to overlook its deep and dynamic meaning. Jesus was really saying this: We are surrounded by a Mind, a Power, an Intelligence, or a Principle that receives the impress of our thought and acts upon it exactly as we think. Our thought is like an object held in front of a mirror. The mirror will always reflect the object exactly. The Law of Mind, like a mirror, reflects back to us what we think.

Now we come to our second proposition: We are thinking and active centers in this Mind, and the sum total of all our thoughts is either silently attracting our good to us or repelling it from us. This shows the part that we are to play in our use of the Power greater than we are. It is the sum total of all our thinking that we must consider. In doing this one of the first things we learn is that ninety percent of our mental activity is unconscious.

The subconscious mind is a storehouse which retains all the thoughts and memories we have ever had. It is this subconscious storehouse of memory, previous acts and thoughts and emotional reactions to life, that psychologists deal with. Our success or failure, our happiness or misery, is largely determined by the content of the subconscious.

In other words, scientific investigation verifies what we are talking about. Most of our thinking is unconscious. Here is where habit patterns of thought are laid down from infancy, and the whole purpose of applied psychology is to find out what these thought patterns are, and, when they are unhappy or morbid or filled with fear, change them so that the natural, normal flow of the Life Force shall be resumed.

Of course we have no controversy with the psychologist. We follow him as far as he goes, but we do add something to his philosophy for we believe that there is a universal Principle of Mind which is always reacting on our thinking, whether it be conscious or unconscious. We really are attracting or repelling the good we desire according to the whole body of our thought.

We come now to our third idea, that we can change our thinking, and, in so doing, cause the Law of Mind to act affirmatively for us instead of negatively. It may seem astonishing, but Jesus actually gave us a technique for this, and perhaps the greatest technique ever given, because he understood all these things probably better than we do. He implied that many of our beliefs are changed only through prayer and fasting, through meditation, and perhaps quite a bit of effort, in which, of course, he was right. He said that we had better pray without ceasing. He also said it would be well if our conversation were "Yea, yea," and "Nay, nay." In light of what we know today about the way the mind works, this was a perfect idea, because Jesus was implying that we are either affirming our good or denying it, and that the thing we greatly fear as well as that which we have faith in can come upon us.

But Jesus added something else. He told us that when our faith is in the good it will automatically obliterate evil; that is, good and evil are not equal powers. Good always overcomes evil. The affirmative attitude will always overcome the negative. Modern psychology has proved this, too, and that is why many psychologists tell us we should accentuate the positive and forget the negative. Just keep on thinking about peace and let confusion go. Affirm the good and forget the evil. This is a sound teaching.

We really are surrounded by a creative Law of Mind which reacts to our thinking. The sum total of all our thinking really decides what is going to happen to us. We actually can change our thinking and cause the very Law that limited us to bring us freedom. What more could we ask? What more could be given than this?

Jesus said: "If ye know these things, happy are ye if ye do them." So let us proceed to the doing. Going back to our first proposition, that we are surrounded by a Law of Mind which acts creatively on our thinking, let us see if we cannot make this the basis of our belief. Do we really accept that there is a self-operating Power around us, a Power which actually can and will do whatever ought to be done for us, if we believe in It? Do we really accept that the sum total of our thinking does decide what is going to happen to us?

We must believe. But since it is natural to believe and to have faith, when we find that we lack these qualities we now know what to do about it, because belief and faith are mental attitudes. So we should practice affirming daily: "I do have faith. I do have conviction. I do believe. I do know and understand that there is a Power greater than I am. I do realize I can use It; there is nothing

34

in me that can doubt, deny, or limit this Power; my whole being accepts It, both consciously and subconsciously." In this way we shall be preparing our minds to pray affirmatively, which means to pray effectively.

This is probably the most important single thing we can do in preparing our minds to launch on the great adventure of dynamic spiritual self-expression, because the whole basis of our thought, and the whole principle of the way it acts, is involved. If there is a Principle of Mind that reacts to our thinking or to our belief, then it naturally follows that if we say, "It cannot," then It cannot because we do not let It. If we say, "It will not," then It will not because we do not permit It. If we limit It to a little good It will not give us a greater good. The Power Itself is absolute; the way we use It is relative. Getting back to the words of Jesus, this is what he meant when he said that it is done unto us as we believe.

The first thing is to be certain that we do believe. Science, revelation, intuition, and experience teach that we may believe, and there is no reason why we should not. John Haldane, the great British scientist, said that science has only discovered one thing that is creative and that is mind. This is why Jesus based his whole thought about God and man and human destiny upon the simple necessity of our belief.

We can practice believing because thoughts are things and when we say, "I believe," and, "There is no doubt in me" we do two things: We affirm our belief, and by so doing build a positive acceptance in the mind at the same time that we reject our doubts by denying them. This is the way thought works. Realizing that ninety percent of our thinking is unconscious, we should daily affirm that there is nothing in us that denies the good we affirm; that every experience we have ever had up until now which denies that good is wiped out of our memory as a negative force; that we are forgiven our mistakes and encouraged to go on and do better.

Now we are ready to see if we cannot actually bring ourselves

THE PHILOSOPHY OF JESUS

to believe that we possess the good we desire even though we do not see any possible way for it to happen. This also can be reduced to a simple method. We can say, "I do accept this good. I do believe my prayer is answered. I do affirm the presence of love, friendship, happiness, prosperity, health, peace — whatever the need may be — and nothing in me denies, rejects, or refutes it. I do accept it."

After we have done this for a while there will come a gradual acceptance of our affirmation. We will learn that as the subjective reactions of our thought build up an affirmative attitude, things will begin to change in our environment. It may take a little time, but we now have courage, knowing that we are dealing with a definite Principle and that It cannot fail.

Sometimes when we try to reverse our whole thought process we find it is a little difficult, for the old negative thought patterns come to the surface and deny us the right to think affirmatively, the right to use this great, silent, invisible, creative Power for definite purposes.

Sometimes when a negative thought arises, if we say, "It isn't so. You have no power; you have no reality; you have no existence," that particular negation will instantly dissolve. Or we may try another method and instead of denying its existence, affirm the opposite. Then we will find the negation gradually disappearing. By experimenting we can discover how to meet the denials of life and gradually convert them into great affirmations.

This should never be done with any sense of morbidity or struggle, or in any sense that we are fighting an opposing force, but rather, with a calm, peaceful, inward assurance, because we know what we are doing and why; we understand how the Law of Mind works; we know how to use It and we are, perhaps for the first time, applying It for definite purposes. We are experimenting but we are experimenting with the fundamental Law of our own being, the Law which we believe finally governs everything in our life. So we are doing something not only worthwhile, but some-

EFFECTIVE PRAYER

thing which should be very interesting.

We are all surrounded by a certain amount of skepticism and doubt, and perhaps many people think that this is all nonsense. That should not bother us in the least. We should know that we are working independently with God and the great Law of Cause and Effect. Whether we are working for ourself, our family, our friends, or the whole world, every affirmative spiritual statement we make will have some power; an invisible Law will be acting upon it.

We have no one to prove this to but ourself. We have no authority for what we do other than the authority of what happens when we do it. Jesus understood this perfectly and went about proving the supremacy of good in the midst of a world torn with confusion, even as our world is today.

We will have to do the same thing, knowing that we have nothing to give the world unless we have first proved it. The blind cannot lead the blind. But alone with Truth, one man can pass from weakness into strength, from fear into faith, from defeat into success, and from a fear of death into a consciousness of everlasting life.

V

SPIRITUAL HEALING

It has been proved that the larger part of our physical ailments are a direct or indirect result of our thinking, and that we can change our thought patterns. But this does not mean that our physical diseases are in our minds only, or that they are just mental illusions. If we have a pain, we know it. Nor will it do us any good, nor will it heal us, for some thoughtless person to say, "It's all in your mind." If we hurt, we know that we hurt.

I am reminded of the boy who was scratching his head at the dinner table and his mother said, "Son, why do you scratch your head?" He replied, "Because I am the only person living who knows that it itches." This boy was not a philosopher, he was not a scientist, he did not pretend to know all the answers, but I think his reasoning was most satisfactory. He knew that his head itched, and he knew that it relieved it to scratch it. And he was right.

But if you or I had some kind of an allergy that produced a continual irritation at the surface of the body, and we went to a modern physician, the chances are more than even that he would probably tell us that the real cause of our allergy, and the physical discomfort attending it, is an inward emotional disturbance of which we are not even aware. The doctor would not say that it is only in our minds and therefore is of no importance. He would merely be implying that our thoughts and emotions don't come together right; there is an inward turmoil or mental conflict which is causing our physical trouble. Then, very likely, he would suggest that we change our thoughts and feelings in such a way as to uproot the cause of our physical disturbance.

But no doctor can compel us to think constructively; he cannot give us a pill of happiness that will remove all discontent from our minds, nor can he write out a prescription that will keep us from worrying. In modern medicine they do not try to do this. When they feel the seat of our physical troubles lies in the emotions, what they really do is to give us a sort of mental prescription that will straighten out our thinking.

But even here something will be missing unless we add some other factors, which are spiritual in their nature. For no one ever worries if he has a complete sense of security, and no one ever worries if he has a complete faith. In the last analysis, all our thinking is based on our deep convictions about life. We do have physical bodies, and we do have minds. But we are also spiritual beings and it really is the Spirit within us that uses the mind, while, in its turn, the mind reflects or reacts on the body.

The answer to our problem, then, is not in merely saying that it is either all in the body or all in the mind. For while it is true that we can establish a relationship of the mind to the body, there is a deeper truth than this and a more important one, and that is the relationship that our mind has to Life Itself. Our faith in Life has a direct relationship to our belief in the Power greater than we are which we can use. We not only have to establish a right relationship between mind and body; it is equally important that we establish a right relationship between mind and Spirit.

A physician might tell someone with stomach ulcers that possibly the real cause of his trouble is a sense of insecurity. Probably his diagnosis would be correct. But the real and lasting cure is something else again. For if a person is suffering from a sense of insecurity, it is not going to do much good to point out this fact to him unless it is also pointed out that there is a kind of security which is great enough, and deep-seated enough, to overcome his sense of insecurity.

This is something that medicine, as such, does not pretend to touch. It merely points to the fact. But the kind of security that is needed to supply this need is not in a bottle or a pill, nor in any physical application or manipulation. For while all of these are at times necessary, they are but temporary cures and there is a great difference between being temporarily relieved of an irritation and being healed of its cause so it cannot reappear. The physician can relieve us; only God can heal.

We all are rooted in pure Spirit, whether or not we know it. We did not have anything to do with this. We did not create ourselves. But we do seem to have pretty well messed up what God has made, and we seem to have this privilege. However, it so happens that our roots do lie in the Spirit, and in most cases what we really need is a healing of the mind even more than a healing of the body.

If it can be established that the mind produces such a large proportion of our physical troubles, and that changing our mental and emotional reactions to life can heal them, then at the same time we are establishing another fact which we are apt to overlook: We have created all our mental patterns and there is nothing in the mind that has not been put there. All our habit patterns of thought have been unconsciously laid down, probably over a period of many years. What we really need, then, is a spiritual healing of the mind. We may have the assurance from modern science, from medicine, and from psychology, that we are not laboring under an illusion when we say that if we permit the Spirit to heal the mind, the mind will react on the body.

If a sense of insecurity, the emotion of fear and the feeling that we are inadequate to cope with life, can produce disastrous results in the body, then it becomes necessary for us to find something that will remove this feeling of insecurity and inadequacy. No one ever yet has been able to supply this need out of the human mind alone — and no one ever will be able to. For just as a tree cannot live without its roots or bear fruit without drawing on the invisible source of its life, so we cannot hope to be well, whole, or happy until we learn to draw on the invisible forces of the Spirit which are around us and within us.

We know that the Spirit already is perfect, and it is only reasonable to suppose that what God has made must be as perfect as God is. There is a spiritual body in which every organ, action, and function of our physical being is rooted and from which it draws its life, and we should readjust our thinking to include the idea that every action of our physical body can be controlled by the Spirit within us.

This in no way denies the physical body; rather, it puts it in its right place. It does not deny the mind or the thoughts we have or the effects they have on the body. It merely puts them in their right perspective. But, beyond and above both mind and body, it introduces the idea of a spiritual person, the God-intended man. And if this God-intended man were not here, you and I would not be here.

What we need is to find the spiritual Idea, the spiritual Reality back of everything. For instance, we speak of people having heart trouble, but what we really mean is that often people have troubled hearts. That is, they have mental and emotional stress and strain which produces a similar effect on this most vital of all organs.

"Jesus said: " . . . Let not your heart be troubled: ye believe in God, believe also in me." When he spoke of "believing in me," of course he meant to believe in the spiritual man, the Christ-Spirit which is within us, not only the Son of the living God but the living Son of God. The spiritual equivalent, then, which can overcome most heart trouble will have to be something that overcomes the troubled heart, the disturbed thought, the inward conflicts with life, the repressions and depressions, and the deep unconscious congestions which the mind has because it is confused and distraught, unhappy and afraid.

The spiritual equivalent of fear is faith. The spiritual equivalent of doubt is certainty. The spiritual equivalent of irritation and agitation and inflammation is peace and poise and calm. The most effective form of mental healing, the most perfect psychology, the most nearly right psychosomatic medicine, is something that reaches deeper even than human experience, something that reaches beyond this little world in which we live and penetrates into that Divine Life by which we live and without which there could be no life.

Spiritual healing is so rearranging our thinking and our reactions to life that they draw on the infinite Source of all being, which is God. This is the office of prayer, of meditation, and of that affirmation of faith to which Jesus said all things are possible. When spiritual mind healing is really understood it will be practiced by everyone, because it is the most natural, normal, and spontaneous thing in the world.

We had to learn to acquire doubts and fears. It took us a long time to create our inner conflicts and emotional disturbances. Truly, they are creations of the human mind. This does not mean that they are unreal or that we can laugh them off, or that we can get rid of them merely by saying they are not there. That is, indeed, poor medicine from any viewpoint, and inadequate. If the physician finds a deficiency in the human body, he supplies the need. If the psychologist finds an inward emotional disturbance, he tries to straighten it out. But how can the picture be complete until we also discover the true relationship that the mind has to the Spirit? We shall find many deficiencies in the mind which only the vitamins of faith and hope and assurance can supply.

It may take time to do this, and effort. It may take the will to be well and the determination to think straight and the courage to face the immediate emergency with a calm trust and a deep and abiding faith. This is something that no one can give to us but ourselves, but each has the power within himself to do this. This is what spiritual mind healing really means.

In actual practice we take certain statements or thoughts or affirmations, and meditate on them until the mind, both consciously and subconsciously, comes to complete agreement, then the mind becomes calm and peaceful and no longer agitated. Then we mentally identify ourselves with the Spirit. This is why we say, "There is one Life, that Life is God." But this statement is not complete until we add: " . . . that Life is my life now." This is what we mean by identifying oneself with God or finding oneself in God. At first this statement may not have much effect, but daily repeating such statements, and trying to feel their meaning inwardly, can produce a transformation of one's entire life. At times this transformation is instant and permanent. But such times are rare, and we need not depend on the inspiration of such a moment, for always the calm, persistent following of this method will finally produce results. No one can change his whole thinking in a moment, but if he knows that he is working with the great Reality, then he has the courage to go on. If he gains a little every day he is content because he knows he is on the road that ultimately will lead to success.

Spiritual healing is an established fact in human experience. It follows a definite Law of Mind. The pioneering work in this field has been pretty well completed and we may accept it as true and valid. What we need now is the application, and this is something each may do for himself, perhaps better than anyone else could do for him. There are no particular formulas for doing this. It is a matter of always trying to reach back to the Spirit within us, always trying to sense Its presence and Its action through us, always believing that It is there, and never denying It.

How wonderful it is to realize that we have access to such a Presence and such a Power. How wonderful it will be when we all draw closer to this Presence and Power in thought, in word, and in feeling. When the day comes that the majority of people on earth do this, a new race will walk this planet.

VI

THE SPIRIT WITHIN

People are the most interesting things in the world. While it is true that we do not always get along with others as well as we might, it is also certain that we could not get along without them. We need each other more than we realize. The world is made up of people, and human relationships are merely reactions of people to each other. Many business firms maintain human relations departments for the purpose of helping people to appreciate each other and get along together in their work.

Psychology tells us that the two things people are most interested in are love and personality. This is not strange because everyone wants to love and be loved; everyone wants to feel needed; everyone wishes to feel that he plays an important role in life. All are attracted to the person who has a winning personality. Thousands of books have been written on this subject and perhaps hundreds of thousands of people have taken courses to be taught how to develop a winning personality. But there are millions of others who neither had the opportunity of reading these books nor of taking these classes. I am sure that they, too, wish to enlarge their circle of friends and their personal influence in the activities in which they are engaged.

That there is a Power greater than we are which is available to us is based largely on the words and the works of the outstanding personality of the ages. It is interesting, then, for us to find out what Jesus taught about personality.

In many ways Jesus was the greatest individual who ever lived. Yet there was nothing arrogant in his teaching. He taught a simple and direct approach to God and to others, which at first looks as though it were a false humility. Yet we find him facing the political, the military, and the ecclesiastical powers of his day with calm assurance. We find him facing death with such a certainty of life that among his last words there was nothing bitter or resentful. They were merely: "Father, forgive them, for they know not what they do," and "Father, into your hands I commend my spirit."

It is this Spirit within us that Jesus was talking about that you and I are interested in. For one thing is certain: Whatever our personality may be, or whatever it is to become, is wrapped up in this one idea — that there is a Spirit in man and that God Himself is incarnated in every living soul. This Spirit within us is the gift of heaven and without it we would not be alive. It is a recognition of this Spirit within us that is the true starting point for the development of personality.

We have often patterned our lives after the lives of others. And yet, Emerson told us that imitation is suicide, that every man should watch the spark of genius that flashes across his own mind, and trust it. Personality, no matter how winsome it may be, or how convincing, or how dominant, is more than a mask we wear, for it is a manifestation of an inner, hidden principle, a Divine spark within us which uses both the mind and the body for its own self-expression.

We could think up all the beautiful things to say or the wonderful and best method of approaching people, and study all the arts of personality development that have ever been taught, and still fall flat on our faces as far as the real personality is concerned. For personality is the flowering of the Spirit within us, the coming forth of a secret relationship that we have with God. The individuals who have greatly influenced the human race throughout the ages are those who have known this and who have made but little effort to influence others. They are the ones who have had the deepest feeling of the Divine Presence within them.

But someone might say, "I don't wish to make a mark on history. I don't feel myself capable of becoming a great leader or a dominant factor in social or political or commercial life. All I want is just to be happy and get along with people and have them like me." And such a one would be right. For the development of real personality must be something that attracts to itself everything necessary for its well-being, which is love and friendship, right human relationships and success, and happiness.

But those who make personal ambition their main approach to life always seem to fail. Again we are privileged to go back to one of the fundamental thoughts of Jesus, who also knew what our human needs are and never belittled them. He said that all these things will be added if we discover the real secret of life and first uncover within ourselves something that we did not even put there, something that we might call the hidden Self.

No one will ever be satisfied, happy, or secure in just developing a dominant personality. For those who try to win their way through life by force some day become weary with the struggle — a mad ambition the end and aim of which never reaches its final goal. Personality is not an external thing at all, for everything we think and say and do, and everything that we appear to be outwardly, is always a result of some hidden fire burning at the center of our being, some Divine Reality which we did not create but which we may discover. I think we can say without hesitation that the person who finds himself in God will discover, at the center of his own being, something which dominates without effort, something which does not have to assume a false front, something which, by the very nature of its being, is both human and Divine.

But someone may say, "But now you are introducing religious ideas that we don't want to be bothered with. What we want is something that can take us into the activities of life in a triumphant manner." This is both right and wrong. Right in that we wish to be successful in living; wrong if we think that of ourselves we can add to or take from what God already has given. For while we can, and should, develop an outer personality, back of this there is something we never thought up — we did not plan it, we did not create it. Finding this something is like exploring a new land which already existed before we discovered it. There are heights and depths to our own being which we have not plumbed.

Our psychological personality, with all its emotions, feelings, actions and reactions, is real enough but behind it there is something more. It is this something more that should be the starting point for the development of the psychological personality. There is a Spirit in man because God is incarnated in everything. But this Spirit has made each one of us just a little different in order that there may be a variation in life.

Why, then, should we expect that any two individuals must be alike? We should not even believe that they ought to or can be identical. We should not study to be alike, but rather, to develop what we really are. Unity does not mean uniformity. Our unity with other people never means that we must think and act as they do. All it means is that we should get along with them. We should unify with everything, while, at the same time, keeping intact and whole that God-given something at the center of our being which is the real Self.

It is, then, to find our true center that is the end and aim of our search — this Divine Person within us and within everyone, which, in a sense, has one hand placed in the hand of God and the other outstretched to humanity. The one who finds himself in God will discover God in others. He will look through different eyes than the one who thinks that he is alone. He draws a strength and an inspiration from Life Itself, for no man can live without God and be whole.

Jesus was a dominant personality; he was the most triumphant person who ever lived because he had discovered his true nature, that part of him which was rooted in pure Spirit, and revealed the strength and the power and the peace of this invisible Presence which we call God.

Since everything is included in God — for God must be the only Presence and Power that there is or else nothing could exist — the person who wants to make the most of himself will have to be the one who has discovered more of himself in that which is greater than he is. Our capacity to think, to live, and to move, or to do anything, is nonphysical and nonmaterial. There is an invisible Self hidden within us which has Its source in a higher Reality and which thinks through our minds, expresses through our actions, and reveals Itself in what we are.

Because this is true there must be at the center of our being a Divine Person, a unique incarnation of God. This is the source of all real inspiration; here, and here alone, at the center of our being, is the real creative power. The question is whether or not we are living from this center, or whether we are thinking of ourselves as detached, separate, divided, alone, and inadequate. Each of us has such a center, and we all have direct access to the infinite Presence, the universal Person. Jesus called this the Father within us, and there could be no more beautiful thought than this, that the Divine Spirit Itself, infinite as It is, is also within us.

We want to find some direct and simple approach to this, the center of all inspiration and all power. Then we want to live from it, think and act and move from it. This does not mean that we have to retire from the ordinary activities of life or repress our personalities as though they were unworthy. Quite the reverse. We shall carry this vision with us into every activity. It will become the power back of all our actions. It will appear in our relationships with others. We shall be more ourselves. Realizing that this Divine center within us is Love, and that the same center exists in others, we shall meet people in love and with consideration, and they will feel something flowing from us — something that cannot be weighed or measured or that we can say looks like this or that or something else. It really is something that is felt but not seen.

Realizing that this Divine center within us, the real person, is an individualization of the Spirit Itself, we shall not be weary; work will become play. Realizing that this center within us is pure affirmation, we shall have no fear. The wonderful thing about it all is the simplicity of it, the directness. Every person should take time to become acquainted with himself; to find God in the only place he can find Him, and to explore this inward, largely unknown country — the Divine center in the depths of every man's mind.

But how could we do this unless we were first convinced that it really is there? We cannot act as though something were true unless we first believe it. This is why Jesus laid such great stress on the need of our believing, of our having faith, of our accepting that we are one with God. With this acceptance of God there must come an acceptance of our real Self that blossoms in our relations with others and finds fruition in its own action.

VII

HEAL THYSELF!

It has been discovered that seventy-five percent or more of our physical ailments are due to inner emotional disturbances. It has also been found that eighty-five percent of our accidents are brought about because of our inner conflicts. And, of course, we all know that our dealings with others mostly depend on our mental attitudes. Whether or not we are happy and contented and have an inward sense of peace, poise, and security, of necessity must be a result of the way we think.

It is easy enough, then, to let these problems answer themselves. For, if we can be whole inside, we will not have to worry very much about what happens outwardly. When we are rightly adjusted to life, living seems to adjust itself to us.

One of our main troubles is that when we are confronted with difficulties we are prone to feel that circumstances are against us or that the trouble lies with other people and not with ourselves. It takes a well-rounded person to be willing to admit that he brings most of his troubles on himself. But this is the starting point of a well-ordered life, and we may as well admit it, and, if necessary, begin all over again, not trying to adjust things and people to our way of thinking, but trying to adjust our own thoughts and feelings so we will harmonize with others and fit into our environment.

In a certain definite sense every man is a physician to his own mind, to his own body, and to his own affairs. The chances are more than even that should we go to a modern physician for a physical diagnosis he would explain that there are certain fundamental emotional attitudes toward life that everyone must have if he expects to remain whole and healthy. If we were to go to someone who has made a study of human relations and tell him that we are out of sorts with our environment, he would not try to change our environment for us, because this he could not do, but he would show us how to adjust our own thinking to that environment. For all human relations simmer down to the art of getting along with others.

If we were in business and hired an expert to analyze what we were doing and perhaps show us how to do it better, he might point out certain wrong adjustments, particular situations, which could be corrected only by a new viewpoint. This leads us right back to the self, to that something inside us which is the arbiter of our fate, and to the way we are using certain laws in nature which govern everything.

We have always spoken of Jesus as the Great Physician, the one who could point out the reason why we have difficulties. If Jesus were the Great Physician, then it was because there were certain adjustments that he must have made to life and to living. This was the result of his communion with the Spirit — he had harmonized himself with Life. He had formed a partnership with God. He had plumbed the depths of human existence and human experience and had discovered that there is a spiritual Reality at the center of every man's being, a Divine Presence and an infinite Wisdom that can and will lead, guide, and direct, when we let It.

We think of Jesus as the most inspired man and the greatest spiritual teacher who ever lived, and we are right. But there is something else that we may have overlooked. Jesus had a spiritual common sense and logic which history has never been able to refute and human experience cannot deny. For instance, Jesus said:

"Consider the lilies of the field, how they grow; they toil not, neither do they spin. And yet I say unto you, That even Solomon in all his glory was not arrayed like one of these." He also told us to consider the birds of the air and the beasts of the field, how they live and travel about and find food and shelter by some Divine direction which flows through them like blood flowing through our veins. And he said: "Wherefore, if God so clothe the grass of the field . . . shall he not much more clothe you, O ye of little faith?"

This really is uncommon common sense, for Jesus was merely saying this: There is a Divine Intelligence that created you. There is a Divine Law that governs all creation. There is a Presence at the center of everything, or else nothing could be here. He said that if you search deep into your own nature you will discover that this Presence is within you as well as around you. It already knows why you are here and what you are and how you should act. It already knows what is best. But you are refusing to accept Its guidance. Every time you deny Its presence you limit Its action through you. Every time you deny Its guidance you limit your own ability to know what is best. Every time you deny Its presence in others you separate yourself from them.

The whole thing is so simple and direct yet so immediate, so close to us, that it has not seemed possible that the inspiration and the power and the direction we know we need are accessible to us. But when we stop to think the whole thing over and give it due consideration, we are compelled to admit that a Power greater than we are governs everything and an Intelligence higher than ours guides.

We wish to live life in its fullness. But how true it is that mostly we rush hither and thither looking for something to heal us, looking for a power to make us whole, whether it be physically or mentally or emotionally, or whether it has to do with our affairs so that we may live successfully. We are all looking for a physician outside us.

And yet, if we were to go to a doctor he would tell us that he is simply making certain physical adjustments in the body which enable nature to take its own course and restore us to health. If we were to go to a psychiatrist he would tell us that he is merely making certain adjustments in our thinking and in our emotional reactions to life which would enable nature to restore a normal balance. And should we go to a personal relations adviser all that he could do is to help us to readjust our thinking so that we will get along better with other people.

In other words, all of these people, as good and necessary as they are and as much as we need them, will concur in this: "We are helping you to heal yourself," or, "We are helping you to get in a position so that nature, or the Power greater than you are, can flow through your thought and body and actions in an unobstructed manner." They are really giving us instructions reading: "Physician, heal thyself. We will do everything we can to help you. Out of our experience we will show you what is wrong and how you can adjust yourself to a better way of living. But of ourselves we do not have the power of life. We cannot give life to you; we cannot give happiness to you; we cannot present you with success, for the simple reason that Life has already made you these gifts. You have already inherited the power to live, but you have not adjusted yourself to it."

If, then, every evidence of science and common sense and human experience points to the fact that we must each become our own physician, we had better accept the fact and see what we can do about it. For no one really wants to be poor or unhappy or sick. There is not a normal person living who does not wish to get along with others and have them like him. And I have never yet met anyone who does not wish to be happy.

In certain experiments which a group of psychologists tried with pigs, they placed the feed trough just outside a heavy wire fence so the pigs could see it and smell it and almost get their noses into it, but not quite. In a short time the pigs became frustrated because they could not get at the food they could see and smell. This frustration became so great that when they finally removed the wire fence and the trough with the food in it was accessible, the pigs simply lay right down beside it and made no attempt to eat. They seemed to have lost even the desire to eat. It is a funny thing to think of pigs having nervous prostration, but this is what happened.

Well, you and I are not pigs, but the lesson applies, for we, too, have erected a wire fence, a barrier, without even knowing it, between ourselves and the Source of our being. A Chinese sage once exclaimed: "O man, having the power to live, why will ye die?" We add to this: "O man, having the capacity to be happy, why will you be unhappy? Possessing the intelligence to know what to do, why do you continue in your mistakes? Having the ability to get along with others, why are you surrounded by discord?"

The pigs had lost the will to try; they had lost the ambition to make another attempt. This is what frustration is. They were stopped. And the poor animals did not have the ability to sit down, like the prodigal of old, and think things over.

But we are different. We do have the ability to analyze the situation and find a solution. But we must also have the will to do this; we must have the imagination to see how it can be done; and we must have a faith to believe that when it is done everything will be well with us.

Since there are no pills that we can take that will produce happiness; since there is no medicine that can give us peace of mind; and since there is no physical manipulation that can give us faith, we must look for a different kind of medicine. We must look for it in the only place it can be found — within ourselves. We are the physician. We must heal ourselves.

But there is something we must remember. We are some part of the Divine Life. There is within each one of us a spark of Divinity. It is this original Thing within us that we must become adjusted to, for all of our thoughts and actions flow from It. This is why

THE PHILOSOPHY OF JESUS

Jesus told us that we should seek the kingdom of God first.

Jesus was able to heal others because he had first healed himself. He was able to direct others because he had first received direction from the Divine Source within himself. He was able to tell others about the kingdom of God because he lived in it. The starting point, then, of our new outlook on life must be that we have direct access to an Intelligence that can guide us, a Life Force or Energy or spiritual Something that can heal us, and a Law of Mind that we can use. This is the starting point.

We may call this faith, hope, religion, or spiritual enlightment — they all mean the same thing. The starting point is to recognize that we are one with God, here and now, and to come to realize that there is a Law of Mind which can bring any desired result about, provided it is constructive. When we were children we had this natural belief, and as we grew up and met experiences that denied the simple faith of the child, we got farther and farther away from the inward center of the child, until finally our frustrations accumulated, and, like the pigs, we refuse even to try again. So we have to start all over and experience some kind of a new birth, a real and actual conversion.

Probably this has been the power and the vitality of every religion the world has ever known, for no matter what form they have taken they have all believed in something greater than the human. Basic religion, rightly understood, is more than a sentiment. It is more than just some happy attitude or outlook toward life. It is more fundamental than this. It is a blending of the human with the Divine, a coming together of our minds with the Cosmic forces that surround us, a conscious union of the soul with its Source, an at-one-ment with God.

We all need a religion, a faith, that will rekindle within us the hope that has been lost, the fire that has been extinguished, the light that has dimmed. We should not be afraid of religious convictions or look upon them as weak or without meaning. For a man without the hope born from faith and the conviction coming from an inward assurance is like a ship without a rudder tossed about by wind and wave.

When we go to a physician for a physical diagnosis, if we are intelligent we will follow his direction. We will follow his course of treatment until we get results. The Great Physician, too, had a certain prescription— instruction— that we should follow, leading back to the one central thought: Get rid of your doubts and fears; discharge from your thought every negative attitude that denies you a right to live in harmony with life and with people; through faith tie your mind back to the Mind of God, and in action live as though you were guided by a supreme Intelligence.

I wonder how many of us are following this Divine prescription, written two thousand years ago by the Great Physician?

VIII

INTUITIVE WISDOM

We are told by child psychologists that fears are acquired. What has happened to us since our infancy that has produced so many fears and uncertainties? It is the endeavor of modern psychology and psychosomatic medicine to go back into our mental and emotional life and discover the blocks, the inhibitions, the repressions and conflicts that hinder the spontaneous flow of peace and joy and creative self-expression.

A man once lived whose wisdom went way beyond our modern knowledge and he told us that if we could keep alive the child in us we should discover the road to peace and happiness and creativity. Jesus said that unless we become as little children, we cannot hope to enter into the kingdom of God. And, of course, the kingdom of God means a life of harmony; it means a life of peace and security and happiness; it means a life of self-expression and love, and it must mean a life filled with enthusiastic zest for living.

We must not overlook another important part of the teaching of Jesus, for he was more than an idle dreamer, he was a practical person. He also told us of a spiritual Power which we can use for definite purposes. One of the mistakes we have made has been to think that Jesus came to save our souls for a future state. While it is true that he was always pointing to this future state, because he knew that we are immortal beings, it is also true that he told us that we should live as though this future state was already here. He taught that there is a way of life which, while it prepares us for an expansion of our being beyond the grave, also includes the expansion of our being while we are here in this world. He linked earth with heaven, time with eternity, and the now with the hereafter.

Nothing is wrong with Life Itself. What seems to be wrong is the way we are using It. Jesus knew what he was talking about when he said that we should relearn to have the simple faith and trust with which we were born, then everything will be well with us.

Everything would be all right if we understood it. Life is for us, even though we use the laws of nature wrongly. The beginning of real wisdom, the starting point of really knowing how to live, is to realize that every man's experience emanates from himself, while his life emanates from God; and that every person has the power within himself to reconstruct his thinking in such a manner that peace of mind, happiness, and joy in living will follow.

The simplest propositions are always the most difficult to understand, and often that which is the most obvious completely eludes us. We are too apt to seek roundabout methods and pathways; too apt to build up obstructions and barriers that nature has never put in our way and that really exist only in our own minds. But these mental reactions we can control because we created them. What we have made we can unmake; what we have created we can recreate. If God, who is the final arbiter of all human fate, has seen fit to put us here, we may be certain that it was for the purpose of expressing life to the full.

We may be certain that we were intended to be happy. We may be sure that everything of a discordant nature in our lives has been introduced and was never placed there by the Divine Will; it is of our own creation. Not that you and I, as individuals, thought up or planned all the evil in the world; rather, we suffer from a gradual accumulation of the ages.

But if we can get two fundamental propositions firmly in our minds we shall find a fresh starting point. The first proposition is that God is Life, God is love, and desires only that which is right. The second is that we have obstructed the passage of Divine Life and Love through us and led ourselves astray by a misunderstanding of the whole meaning of our relationship with God and with each other.

If we were to say to the average person, "Beauty is in the eye of the beholder," he might say, "Look at all the ugliness in the world. Look at all the evil. Look at the unhappiness and confusion. How can you say that either beauty or harmony is in the eye of the beholder?" Here we are up against a real practical proposition, and this practical proposition is ourselves. Are we able to see peace in the midst of confusion? Are we able to reach out and feel the Divine Presence in the midst of everything that contradicts It?

There is a story in the Bible which says that a group of men who were fighting for the Lord saw their enemies, who greatly outnumbered them, and suddenly they became afraid and would have retreated in great confusion except for a "still small voice," the voice of the prophet of God, which told them to look up. As they looked up they beheld vast throngs fighting on their behalf. They saw a Power that could completely vanquish their enemies; they felt a Presence surrounding them which would give them perfect protection. Seeing this, they were no longer afraid of the enemy and the victory of right was gained over wrong.

This is a simple story but it is not to be passed off merely as a beautiful word picture, for it has within it an element of deep reality — the final victory of truth over error. This is what we are confronted with in the world today. This is why it is necessary, as never before, that a great new vision come to us, a hope and an assurance that right is might, that the power of good can vanquish its foes, and that truth crushed to earth will rise again.

Yes, beauty is in the eye of the beholder, if he sees it. And peace can come out of confusion, if we listen to peace instead of confusion. This applies not only to the individual life but to the life of the whole world, for the world itself is merely a great mass of individual lives joining their hopes and fears and aspirations in one common accord.

It is written that the nation without a vision shall perish from the face of the earth, and we know that an individual without a vision perishes daily. But if we can come to believe that most of our troubles are self-imposed, that they were never really intended to be, and if we can have complete conviction that there is a Presence and a Power which is always on the side of right, then we shall have the courage to start all over again. No single individual or nation ever existed that finally won out against the power of good.

We are individuals and we shall have to start with the self. Beauty and peace and joy really are in the eye of the beholder and life belongs to the one who lives it and gladness sings in the heart of one who is glad. We shall have to start with ourselves and somehow or other find our way back to the innocence and the peace and the joy of those days which knew no trouble, those times which had no fear, because we felt the protecting presence of our human parentage. We must feel the guidance of love and wisdom and the security and joy that come only from a sense of belonging to the Universe and from a feeling of trust and faith in a Power greater than we are.

We had this when we were children, and then as we began the slow and tedious and sometimes heartbreaking process of growing up, we all but lost that early vision when the world was our world, when everything was for us and nothing against us. Whether we accept the simple proposition of Jesus, which is by far the best of all, or the slower processes of modern psychology which painfully and laboriously take us back in our imagination to a place of security within, through what they call self-awareness, we shall arrive at the same conclusion.

Personally, I think the proposition of Jesus should be accepted in all its simplicity, and I know that those who do accept it automatically overcome the psychological and emotional barriers just as though they were not there. Life is to each one of us what we make it. We shall find joy if we really look for it, and we shall discover happiness wherever we go if we carry happiness with us.

Let us take another thought of Jesus when he said that we should not be too concerned about the outside of things, but "cleanse first that which is within the cup and platter," by which, of course, he meant our inward lives, our thoughts, our emotions, our feelings, our mental reactions to everything around us, and above everything else, our ideas about God and the destiny of our soul and the relationship we have with each other. For it is this inside of ourselves that is meant by the eye of the beholder.

Why could we not, without anyone's help, learn to analyze our own thinking, find out just what our reactions to life are, and why, and make a real business of reeducating our minds until finally all our reactions become positive and constructive, hopeful and helpful? But always with this added thought in mind: no one does, or possibly can, live by himself alone.

We should start with this idea: Life is living Itself in us and through us. We are a part of It. That Life which entered into us has never separated Itself from us; It is merely waiting our conscious cooperation with It. Always there is a Presence with which we may commune. Always there is a Power greater than we are that we can call on. And always God is for us, provided, of course, we are for God. We cannot expect God to be for us if we are trying to oppose or go contrary to that which is the very Essence of harmony and love and beauty and reason. But we can make up our minds to retrace our mental pathway back to the place where we started with only God, symbolized at first through our human parents and now broadened and deepened by the realization that we had not only earthly parents but that we also have a heavenly Parentage.

Why should we not retrace the pathway of our lives until it leads back to the place of childlike confidence in living and then, as it were, grow into adulthood all over again, ever keeping this thought in mind: "The Spirit is daily flowing through me into action. It is daily projecting Itself through me in my relations with others. The Wisdom of the Spirit is guiding me. The Power of the Spirit is guarding me. The Presence of the Spirit goes before me and makes perfect my way."

Since we cannot live by ourselves alone, we must maintain the same attitude toward others. We must come to realize that God is incarnated in everyone. This means that the God we see in others is the same God we recognize in ourselves. If this is what we are seeing, this is what we shall experience.

The person whom we call the hardheaded realist might exclaim that this is just a lot of empty idealism, just a lot of wistful wishing. I would like to ask this person a very simple question: Where have you been leading us? Have you not led us to a place where the trail runs out and stops? Have you not led us up a canyon where the pathway runs into solid granite? Has your pathway led us to the mountaintops where the perennial snows forever melt, and the brooks and the rivers flow down to refresh the valleys and quench the thirst of the desert and cause the waste places to bloom and bear fruit?

No, I am not concerned with the ideas of the hardheaded realist. I am aware that those too few people to whom the world must look for inspiration were more realistic than anyone else because they discovered that for which the whole world seeks — just simple peace of mind, just plain joy in living, just the assurance that everything is not a mistake. They have known that the Power back of all things will do all things well, if we let It.

There is no question but that the world will have to discover its Source. There is no doubt but that we must give God a chance. But to you and to me it will forever remain true that our reactions to life are in our own mind, what we see is in our own eye, and what we experience is our own creation.

IX

INVISIBLE FORCES

It is said that the average man draws on only ten percent of his real capacity; the other ninety percent is submerged and mostly unused. We would think it wonderful if we could multiply our talents ten times. I have no doubt we can do this if we really try.

It is probable that the average person would react to such a suggestion by saying, "How could it be possible that I have so much more talent than I am using? It seems too good to be true."

Let us take a very simple lesson from nature. Perhaps, from where you are sitting you can see a tree in full bloom. If so, remember that the tree's roots from which it draws its life are entirely invisible. Unless the tree drew on this invisible source it would never flourish.

We have roots in the Mind of God. Our personality, our individuality, everything that we are and do that the world sees is really a result, an effect of our invisible forces — forces which are continually drawing on the Infinite. But, somehow or other, in our ignorance we block or limit the flow of Divine Power into our lives.

Of course we do not do this intentionally. We all desire a pleasing personality, we want to make good in life, we want people to like us, and we desire to be worthwhile. But too often when we make an inventory of our assets we count only, and depend only upon, the circumstances that surround us. We say, "How can I better myself? I haven't the power or the personality," or, "I haven't the natural attractiveness that is necessary to making good in life." Right here is where our faith in the Power greater than we are must be brought into play.

It was his great claim on God, or the Power greater than he was, that enabled Jesus, the human being, to become a Divine Man while still living in the flesh.

We must come to believe that the Father does dwell within us, and that this creative Spirit which is back of all things also flows through us. God has need of us or He would not have put us here. The Divine wishes to express through us or we would have no existence. As a matter of fact, we really have no existence of ourselves alone. It is only because we live in God that we live at all. If we think of ourselves as rooted in God, and expect Divine Power to flow through us, every thought we have and our every act will be animated by the same life and power and beauty that clothes the lily of the field. As Jesus pointed out, we would be but following the law of our own lives.

We speak about wonderful personalities and attractive people and people with dynamic thoughts and creative acts, and we admire them. And often we wonder why these people seem to be so endowed. Yet, I have never known a creative person who did not realize that he was drawing upon Something within him which was greater than he was.

I once knew the country's leading cartoonist. The nature of his work was such that he had to create new ideas daily and draw pictures of them for a newspaper syndicate. I asked him how he accomplished so much and he told me that he had a room with four blank walls and the only furniture in this room was a table and a chair; that when he needed ideas he would go into this room, sit down and become quiet. When he looked around at the blank walls there was nothing to sidetrack his attention and he would just sit there and wait for ideas to come to him.

He said that sometimes he would sit there for two or three hours and nothing would happen. Then all at once something would begin to flow from within him — a new thought, a new idea — and he would take a pencil and begin to write his impressions. This is the way his ideas came; his imagination drew upon the invisible Source within which he knew to be God. He would sit there with the mental attitude: "God is giving me ideas and as they come to me I will draw pictures of them." Year after year he produced. There never seemed to be any lessening of the flow, no stoppage of the creative action, and no limit, apparently, to the ideas.

Every creative artist does this, and I am sure every inventor does. Why should not you and I do it? We have to start with the proposition that all things are possible to God; that God makes everything out of Himself by the very simple process of becoming the thing He makes. There is no struggle, no holding of thoughts, no willpower involved.

We often feel that we are only half alive, but because God has implanted something within us which knows more than we do, we live in spite of ourselves. How is it that we eat mince pie or a ham sandwich or maybe a salad, and have it turn into flesh and blood and hair and fingernails? Here is the miracle of life, the invisible becoming visible. We are so used to the process that we never question it; we just accept it, take it for granted. Why could we not take it for granted that God will give us ideas, that the Spirit within us, as Jesus said, knows what we have need of even before we ask?

Suppose every time the tree thought of putting forth a new branch it would say, "How am I going to do it? I only have a certain number of branches. I don't know how to make a new branch." Now, just for the fun of it, let us suppose this tree is a person, just as you and I are, and it is bemoaning its fate because it would so greatly like to have a few more branches, but it does not know how to make them. And thinking of the tree as a person, let us assume that every time the tree says, "I don't know how to make a new branch," it is blocking off the possibility of drawing its life from the soil. If this should happen, then the tree never would make any more branches; it would begin to die from that very moment.

But the tree is not a person. All it does is depend on nature; all that it knows is to grow. So it never short-circuits the Divine Energy that gives it life. But we are people and we can short-circuit the Divine Energy that should be flowing through us. The funny part of it is that we short-circuit It when we deny that It is there. The reason we deny It is because we do not see this Energy. Because we do not see It, we do not believe It is there. If we really believe that all things are possible to God, then we should no longer deny that God knows what to do with His own creation and we should most certainly include ourselves in that creation.

Let us see what would happen to us if we should include ourselves in God's creation. Right at the start we would learn to have a little better opinion of ourselves. I am not talking about an arrogant or conceited opinion for we already have learned that we can do nothing of ourselves; we live because we are drawing on the invisible Source of all life. The only way that God can work for us is to work through us, and God really cannot give us anything unless we take it.

We wish to draw upon this Power, to let our roots run deep into that Life which is already perfect and complete. We want to live happily and without fear, for fear short-circuits the Divine Energy. Confusion and uncertainty cause the very Power which gives us freedom to produce bondage. We should start by accepting ourselves for better or for worse. But in this instance, let us be sure that we accept ourselves for better because we are thinking of that deep, hidden Self, that Self which the Bible tells us is hid with Christ in God.

Here is where prayer and meditation make possible the miracles of life. For prayer is communion with the invisible Presence that presses around us. Prayer is a reaching out and a reaching back to the Divine Life which sustains us. And meditation opens up an avenue in our mind for the outflow of this Life. Remember, we are talking about affirmative prayer, for there should be nothing negative in our communion with God. It should always be affirmative. We should never say that God cannot, or will not, but always that God can and will and does.

As we meditate on these thoughts we should seek to make them real until nothing in us contradicts the Divine fact. We cannot doubt that we are put here to express Life. Jesus said: ". . . I am come that they might have life, and that they might have it more abundantly." Jesus was no crepe hanger. He was a "jubilant and a beholding soul," who knew every moment that God was with him and for him, and he continually relied on his invisible Source. Jesus, more than anyone else we know of, actually believed that spiritual forces existed, and, more than anyone else, he recognized their presence and accepted their power.

Probably we shall have to do some work with ourselves along this line. We shall have to train our minds to have faith and confidence in the good, the enduring, and the true. After having cleared all doubt from our consciousness, we must learn daily to affirm that all the Presence and all the Power — all the Life that there is — is in us and for us and with us.

There is one more thing we certainly should not forget to add: The higher forces of life always work constructively. When we use them constructively there seems to be no limit to their possibility. But the moment we begin to use them destructively, they appear to block themselves. This seems to be the only condition that the Divine has laid down which might be considered limiting. But it really is not limiting at all. We could not expect to use the Law of Mind for evil purposes, nor could we expect through hate to generate love, nor could we hope for God to give us that which we refuse to pass on to others. These are the only conditions Jesus laid down when he told us that we would always receive if we would pray aright.

For example, we can love without limit. We can love everyone and everything and feel kindly disposed toward people and circumstances and situations, and this attitude toward life will never hurt us. It will never dampen our ardor or enthusiasm, nor will it block the flow of Life through us. Rather, it will tend to accelerate it. But the moment we begin to hate, dislike, and oppose, we discover that we are blocking the flow of Life, and gradually these negative attitudes stifle us, they short-circuit the flow of the Energy from the roots of our being into the things we are doing.

It is interesting to realize that when we are on the right track there is no limit, but when we get on the wrong track it runs out and stops, and we are blocked. It seems as though God has imparted His own Life to us, placing no limitation or condition that would restrict us other than this: Our life must be lived constructively, in unity and love and sympathy with everything around us if we expect to live it to the full. I believe that every person is born to be creative and to live to the fullest and enjoy life, to be happy and glad and prosperous and whole, because I do not believe that God is a failure. No, God never makes mistakes. We are the ones who err.

If we are certain that our lives are constructive, and if our whole desire is to live in such a way as to harm no one but to bless all, then I think we should place no limit on the possibilities of our future. Since everyone is an individual, no one can rob anyone else by living as though he were whole and happy and unafraid. There is nothing to be afraid of in God's world, for whether we are here or somewhere else, we may be certain that He doeth all things well.

This great gift of Life is to be accepted, even as the lilies of the field and the birds of the air. Let us try this simple experiment by daily saying to ourselves:

All that the Father hath is mine. God wants me to be whole and happy and well and prosperous. There is nothing in me that can deny His presence, His power, His wisdom, His guidance, and His protecting love. Therefore, today, and every day, I shall live life to the full. I shall sing and dance and be glad. And always within me there is the Presence and the Power — the Life of God. And so it is.

SUCCESSFUL LIVING

Everyone wishes to be a success in life, but real success means more than just having a permanent position in society, in the commercial world, or in any other one walk of life. Real success means happiness and fulfillment in everything we are doing, and it must include enough of "this world's good" that we have a sense of security and well-being.

All these things are contained in the teaching of Jesus. For he said, ". . . your Father knoweth that ye have need of these things."

Jesus did not say that God has prepared a kingdom for us in some future state only. He told us that if we live rightly every good thing necessary to happiness while we are on earth will be supplied, and that as a fitting climax we shall also inherit the kingdom of God hereafter.

But Jesus said more than this — he said that that kingdom which we shall inherit is already here and that we may as well begin enjoying it today. That is why he said that we need not take anxious thought for the morrow, but that we should have such a deep and abiding trust in the Power greater than we are that everything that we need today will be supplied.

We find Jesus going about healing the sick because he knew this was their first need. He fed the multitude when they were hungry and he fed them with the kind of food that sustains physical life. And he did not overlook the need we all have for pleasure in living. At the wedding feast, when they ran out of wine he turned water into wine. In no place do we ever find Jesus separating Life from living. What he really did was to make heaven and earth come together and meet in our present experience. He said that the love and abundance of God's kingdom is at hand — stretch forth your sickle and reap the harvest of God's abundance; permit Him to heal you of your diseases; permit Him to provide everything that you need, for nothing is withheld.

How could it be otherwise? For God is the great Giver. Life comes fresh and new to us every day as though it were saying: "Behold, I have laid the gifts of heaven before you. What are you going to do with them? Do you wish to remain sad and depressed in the midst of an eternal joy? Yours is the choice."

Jesus also told us that we must some day discover that the old forever passes into the new. He told us that we should use everything that we have to the full and not bury our talents in the ground nor hide them lest they become moth-eaten and rust away into nothing. It is as though he had said: Life is a game. Life is continual movement. Life is forever changing. But running through it all, if we learn the secret of living, there is an all-sustaining Law of Mind upon which we may rely. There is a Divine Presence with which we may commune. There is a kingdom of Peace into which we may enter. There is a joy that may be ours, if we live and think and act as though we were in partnership with God, right now.

It is this partnership with the Infinite that we wish to establish. We want to so tune in to the Divine Harmony that all discord will disappear. We want to so unify ourselves with the peace of God that all confusion will leave us. Jesus put the whole thing together and said, in effect: Just think it over.

If we wish people to like us, we must first like them. This takes us back to the old nursery rhyme: " 'Why does the lamb love Mary

74

so?' the eager children cry. / 'Why, Mary loves the lamb, you know,' the teacher did reply." It is interesting, isn't it, that an old nursery rhyme teaches us about the mystery of the kingdom of God. We have to love if we want to be loved.

We want happiness, for there is no success without it. But happiness is a state of mind. If we want to be attracted to happy situations and happy people, we must learn to be radiant within ourselves. The Law of Mind works automatically on our thoughts, and the person who continually tunes into unhappiness will find himself surrounded by unhappiness, thinking that fate is against him. He must reverse his whole process of thinking and then the miracle takes place — he gradually discovers that he is living with happy people because he has become happy himself.

We want success. If we want an Intelligence greater than ours to run our business, then we must believe that there is such an Intelligence, and act and think as though It actually were operating in our affairs and definitely affirm that It is — and affirm, believing.

Do we need money or some other commodity necessary to our well-being? Jesus never condemned this. He said, "Render to Caesar the things that are Caesar's, and to God the things that are God's." Moreover, he implied that when we have rendered unto God the things that are God's, Caesar will be taken care of. First things first — that is all he was talking about. The greater includes the lesser.

If we are confronted with pressing needs it is not always easy to get away from the thought long enough to actually believe that these needs are met. Yet, every such condition that confronts us is but another opportunity to prove the supremacy of the Spirit and the availability of the Law. We want to live more fully and we feel that we should because something within us knows the fullness of life. We want to live more completely and something within us knows that love is the great reality. So, in our prayers and meditations, in our affirmations and denials, we must shift the whole basis of our thinking until the negative reactions no longer rise up in our thought.

As we learn to think in an affirmative manner, we find that the subconscious content of negation gradually slips away and the day comes when it is no longer there. Then it is that the winds of God blow clear from the kingdom of heaven on earth and fill the sails of our hope with a power that takes us into the haven of our desire.

XI

GOD MEETS YOUR NEEDS

We know that we cannot coerce God, nor can we misuse the laws of nature. It is a true saying that the laws of nature obey us when we first obey them. All our inner conflicts are a result of a violation of the natural laws of self-expression. No patient ever came to a psychologist or a physician whose illness did not arise out of a violation, at some point, of a natural law. This is why we say that disease is unnatural, whether it be a physical disease or an emotional or mental one.

As a matter of fact, all that the physician to the mind or the physician to the body does, and all that he attempts to do, is to assist in restoring the natural function of a natural law. All that the physician hopes to do is to help nature to do what she would do anyway, if she were let alone.

Surely, it would be a false statement to say that nature does not wish to keep us well and whole and happy, or is testing us to see how much we can take from life. If we followed this procedure in scientific research we would get nowhere, for the scientist always starts with the idea that there is much more freedom in nature than we have understood, and that when we comply with her laws we shall be liberated from a bondage that nature herself never really imposed on us but was imposed on us by our own ignorance.

It was only a few years ago that the vast Imperial Valley was a waste place, a desert. We did not think it wrong to build dams and change water courses or even seed the clouds and cause them to give us rain. And see the result! The desert was made to blossom and bear fruit.

Here is something we should not overlook: God had already provided everything necessary to produce the abundant crops we now enjoy. Just as soon as we complied with the laws of God, which are laws of nature, the miracle took place. We did not feel that God was testing us or trying to keep us in a state of semi-starvation because the desert had not yielded the harvest until we cultivated it. We took it for granted that it was part of the whole Divine scheme of things that when we did our part, nature would do the rest.

We might have said: Why shouldn't God do it if we let Him? And God did do it — *when* we let Him. But first we had to learn how to put everything together in the right way. As a matter of fact, when we put things together rightly, everything else is automatic. The only difference between the man of ancient times and our own time is that we have learned how better to cooperate with nature.

But there are other desert places in our experience. Too often we are unhappy, mentally unwhole. Too often we lack the good things of life. Is it going too far to say that too often we are burdened with physical diseases that need never have been? The Law of Mind is just as real as other laws in nature, so why should we not find out how It works and learn to comply with It, with the definite end in view that we shall live a fuller and happier life?

But, of course, before we can use this Law we must believe that It really exists and that we are supposed to use It. We should not think of the Law of Mind as something beyond the realm of nature, as something apart from the whole scheme of things. Very often, in our sincere desire to do right and to be right, we are a little afraid to introduce the thought that we are really rooted in pure

Spirit and actually can draw on Divine Power and use It for definite purposes.

We have limited ourselves all too often by thinking that nature's laws extend only as far as we can see. Always the laws of nature have existed universally, if they have existed any place. We could not say that our horizon is the end of space just because it is as far as we can see. There are unlimited horizons, and as we begin to move toward our present horizon we discover it moves back, and it keeps moving back as we go forward. What we all need is the courage to keep moving into new horizons.

We are just beginning to learn that all the laws of the Universe are real and dynamic and creative, and that they can be used for definite purposes. We have at last found a key to the greater possibility — and this key is faith.

We have come to realize that even faith acts like a law. Jesus did not break the laws of nature or of God when he used faith. He merely complied with the higher Law of his being. He did not deny that the paralyzed man needed to be healed; what he did was to use his faith to heal him. He did not say that the multitude was not hungry; rather, he fed them. He did not say that they should not pay a tax to Caesar; he found the money with which to pay the tax. He could not have used his faith as he did if he had not been completely convinced that it was natural and right that God should help us. If we were as sure of our position as he was of his, we could then expect to receive the same answers.

The question naturally arises: Why is it that we are not sure of our position? The answer is simple enough: We have not yet learned to try our faith. We have not experimented with it enough. We have not prepared our minds to accept the simple proposition, not only that all things are possible to God, but that it is also possible for us to cultivate the faith that a Divine Power can and will meet our human needs. Paul boldly proclaimed: "That our faith should not stand in the wisdom of men, but in the power of God."

Right now we are in this position: We do believe in a Power greater than we are and we do believe that It is ready and willing to meet our needs. We are just now beginning to learn how to hook this Power up with what we are doing. We are beginning to understand the relationship of this Power to our belief and to our faith. We are beginning to understand that the way we believe and the faith we use is actually our individual way of using this Power.

This is not a new idea at all, for thousands of years ago it was stated that "as [a man] thinketh in his heart, so is he." But we have so long been walking through the maze of human opinions that we have shrunk our outlook to comply with the wisdom of men and not with the power of God.

The adventure in faith in which we are now engaged is a reopening of the horizon of the power of God. We are beginning to accept the idea, and to use it, by believing certain things in certain ways to get certain results. This is why, even though a man might be afflicted with some physical condition or some physical illness, that we direct him to reach beyond the present condition to believe in perfect health — not only to believe in perfect health, but to believe in it for himself.

Our beliefs are the things that direct the power of the Law of Mind, but we do not get these beliefs that we have by accident. Each and every belief has been formed by previous experience until it has become a habit of thought. Because this is true, we see the possibility of changing our old beliefs and forming new ones until they, too, become a habit of thought. This is what we mean by scientific prayer and affirmative meditation. For, of course, our prayers and meditations do not change the Divine Nature; they merely put us in a position to affirmatively express It. They make us obedient to the Divine Law so that we may use It in everything we do.

We wish to know how we should use this Law of Mind and just what it is that may be obstructing Its affirmative operation through us. In doing this the very first obstacles we come up against are the habits of thought that we have entertained for years, thoughts that deny the possibility of the good we wish to experience, as though something arises from our minds which says, "It's too good to be true," or, "Nothing good could happen to me," or, "I don't understand how to use this Law anyway," or, "I am not good enough to use It."

It is no wonder that the Bible said that a man's enemies shall be those of his own household. But here is a blessing in disguise, for if our real enemies are our own thoughts, we at least have located them, we now know what they are and how they work, and we know that we can change them.

The very fear we have had can be converted into faith, and the misuse of the Law of Mind which has produced bondage can as easily bring about our freedom. We must know that It not only can, It will, because It must. The first thing we have to learn to do, then, is to convert every negative mental attitude into a positive one, every fear into a faith, and every uncertainty into an assurance. The one who does this the best is the one who has the deepest conviction and the most simple and child-like belief in a Power greater than he is.

It was not hard for the early settlers to realize that if they could get water on the desert it would spring forth into fruitage. They understood this well enough and what they had to seek out were the sources from which the water flowed — the deep subterranean passages and the high mountaintops and the clouds that floated over them, and the great will of nature to create.

Let us take this same idea and apply it to our mental and spiritual lives, realizing that nothing can oppose us but our own belief. Let us carefully watch our thoughts and listen to the way our minds are working. Surely we shall be surprised at the negative statements we are making about ourselves and each other and the possibilities of life. We shall be surprised how many times we are denying our good every hour of the day. We shall be equally surprised when, after converting our negative attitudes into positive ones, how easily the Law works for us.

In actual practice we take a few simple statements every day and think about them until they become real to us. For instance, suppose that we awake with this thought: "This is the day that God has made and I am going to be glad in it." And then, when the thought comes up — as it may — "Well, but after all you haven't very much reason to be glad. Just think of all the things that happened yesterday," right here is where we must be on the alert and say, "Yesterday is gone forever. This is a new day."

If we do this we soon discover that when a negative thought rises in our mind, by flatly denying it we can remove its power. When we affirm its exact opposite we not only build up a resistance to the negative thought, we actually convert it into a positive power. For fear and faith are merely two ways of thinking; each uses the same power. So we are not fighting a real adversary but really are rearranging our thinking. If the thought comes that says, "What reason have I to suppose I can be happy and whole today?" we must tie our thought right back to the idea that we are one with God, one with all the Life and Presence and Power there is, and one with the only Law there is — and affirm that God in us is happy.

Why shouldn't God help us? Let us believe, with Jesus, that it is the Father's good pleasure to give us the many blessings of the kingdom of heaven, remembering that Life gives us our blessings through our beliefs and through our thoughts. So we become diligent about the kind of thoughts we think. We are careful to see that the thoughts that flow into our consciousness are thoughts that are like our highest concept of good — thoughts of health, thoughts of beauty, thoughts of peace, thoughts of life. These are thoughts about the kingdom of God and it is the Law of this kingdom alone that can free us from all our fears and set us safe on the pathway to a new life.

XII

COMPLETE ACCEPTANCE

Because we are all human I am sure we all have the feeling at times that our burden is too great to bear; that the load of life is too heavy to carry. How grateful we would be to discover the secret of lifting the burden and placing it on the shoulders of the only Power that knows no burdens.

At first it would seem as though this means an escape from living, as though we might be running away from our problems rather than solving them. This is the last thing we should attempt to do, for we need not deny the reality of problems in order to find their solutions. The greater the problem, the more complete should be its answer. And the greater the burden, the more certain we should be that it can be dissolved.

The Bible clearly states that we should cast our burdens on the Lord, and that we should believe with our whole being, with everything that is within us, that there is a Power which can convert these burdens into freedom and turn our fear into faith and our doubt into certainty. Jesus said, "Come unto me, all ye that labour and are heavy laden, and I will give you rest." Shortly after that Jesus departed from this world, telling his followers that he would send "the Comforter . . . even the Spirit of Truth, which proceedeth from the Father. . . ."

It seems as though Jesus were saying: Watch carefully what I am doing and realize that I am placing my whole reliance on the Father within me. And when I have gone away, when I have left this world, you are to realize that this Father also dwells in you and if you accept His Power It will work for you and your yoke will be easy and your burden will be light.

Jesus knew that he would not forever remain with his followers, and he knew that every man must discover for himself that he, as an individual, has a direct relationship to the Spirit. It was this Spirit, this Divine Comforter, that he said would remain with us forever.

This is what is meant by relying on a Power greater than we are. We are not only operated upon by physical forces in the physical universe, we are also operated upon by spiritual forces in the spiritual Universe. Since the Spirit finally must control everything, including our physical bodies and affairs, Jesus told us that our first approach should be to the Spirit: ". . . seek ye first the kingdom of God . . . and all these things shall be added unto thee."

Jesus did not say that when we seek the kingdom of God everything else will be subtracted. He said it will be added. He knew that we have need of physical things in a physical universe. But another thing he knew which we have not quite understood is that the spiritual can control the physical, and that there are no burdens in the Spirit — there is no sorrow, no grief, no sickness, no despair, no poverty, no unhappiness in God.

It was because Jesus was so consciously aware of the Divine Presence and the operation of the Law in everything he did, and because he so definitely drew upon It, that he was able to do what he did. He proved the power of the Spirit over all apparent resistance. He never denied the things we have need of; he merely affirmed that they will be provided if we join ourselves with the spiritual Cause of everything. This is why he said that his yoke was easy and his burden was light. He had cast all burdens onto the Spirit. But before he did this, he must have come to a complete acceptance, a place of such absolute faith that physical obstructions, no matter what their nature, had no existence for him.

If Jesus had done all this and had said, "I have a power that no one else can possess," he would still have been the greatest man who ever lived. But this is exactly what he did not say. What he really said was, in effect: Because I have done this, you can do it also. The Presence that is around and within me is around and within you. The Power that is with me is with you. The Law that I am using you can use.

Then he carefully told us just what to do to remove every obstruction from the pathway of wholeness: Give, and to you will be given. Love, and you will be loved. Enter into peace and you will become peaceful. Find the joy that I have found and you will be joyful. Arrive at the faith that I have arrived at and you will "know the truth, and the truth shall make you free." Get rid of the burdens of your own mind. Get everything out of your thinking that is afraid or doubts or is uncertain, and then you will find that you already have entered into that kingdom which is forever at hand and within you.

This is the key to the whole situation: You and I have burdens, but God has none. You and I have fears and doubts and uncertainties and worries; God has none of these things. They do not belong to the Divine kingdom, not if Jesus knew what he was talking about. Jesus prayed that this kingdom of God should come on earth even as it is in heaven, and then said it will come to us, as individuals, and to the world as a whole, when you and I and the world rightly interpret Life.

The things we have to get rid of in casting off our burdens are our own negative thoughts and feelings, our own doubts and uncertainties, our own unhappiness and despair. We have nothing to offer God other than our simple and sincere acceptance. God cannot give us what we have need of until we first remove the obstructions in our own minds. For, in a certain sense, Life has already given us everything. But nothing is ours until we use it and even the Divine must wait on our acceptance.

Let us sèe how this works in actual experience. Suppose we are confused and lack peace of mind. There are so many reasons why we are confused, so many reasons why it is impossible to have peace of mind. There is so much that we have to do, so many things we have to attend to, so much unfinished business. We think we are too busy to get still, to become quiet and listen to peace. This is all a mistake. No one is too busy to be made whole.

Peace already exists at the innermost center of everything, and when we become quiet and meditate on peace and thoughts come up in the mind which argue against our being peaceful, these are the burdens that we must unloose. When the thought comes that says there is so much confusion in the world it is impossible for us to become peaceful, we should say: "That is a lie about the Truth. The Truth is that peace exists. I shall no longer listen to the confusion. I am listening to peace."

If we do this, only for a few moments, we will discover that peace seems to envelop us and flow through us. The confusion actually disappears because we have cast our burden of confusion on the Law which knows no confusion. It is as though we threw a snowball in a pail of boiling water and watched it dissolve. The water did not argue against the snowball, and the snowball could not resist the heat of the water. It had no choice other than to melt and become a part of the water. So it is with our fear if we can get still long enough to have faith. The fear then becomes subject to Something greater than it is, an all-powerful and unconquerable Force which dissolves it until finally the fear itself is converted into positive faith.

I certainly am not denying that we have burdens. All I am saying is simply that there is Something that has no burdens, there is Something that knows no confusion, there is Something that has no fear. That Something is already right where we are. Emerson said that we are surrounded by spiritual laws that execute themselves, and added: "For it is only the finite that has wrought and suffered; the infinite lies stretched in smiling repose." All great spiritual geniuses have understood this.

Our trouble is not with Reality or with the Truth; it is with ourselves — our confusions, our doubts, our fears. These we shall have to convert, and it may take time and it may take patience. But how far have we come by adding confusion to confusion, and fear to fear, and doubt to uncertainty, and misery to unhappiness? We do not extinguish a fire by throwing on more fuel.

There is no use for us to wait for things to become better in our outside world, no use to wait for some terrific experience to come to us which will make everything right, no use to wait at all. The place to begin is right where we are, and the time to start is now. The Power already exists, the Law is already operating, the Divine Presence has never left us, God is still in His heaven, and His kingdom is already within us.

I believe that we are surrounded by spiritual Law which executes Itself. I have no doubt at all that Jesus understood this perfectly and used It completely. Nor do I have the slightest doubt but that we can use It. Perhaps we are using It now, in reverse. Perhaps the very faith we have in our fear causes the thing we fear to come into our experience. Perhaps all we have to do is to reverse this process in our own thinking.

It seems to me that this is true and that we are not really dealing with good and evil, but only with one Power which we can use in two ways. But It is a Power which finally delivers Itself to us completely only when we use It for good and constructive purposes. If we can just come to feel that nothing is really against us and everything is for us ("If God be for us, who can be against us?") I believe this would be the supreme affirmation, the complete abandonment of our faith to spiritual Law.

This is the experiment you and I are embarked on. This is the thing we wish to prove above everything else. This is, it seems to me, the great lesson which the world needs. So we should enter into this experiment with joy. We should have a great surge of thankfulness and there should be a complete and childlike trust and faith. Such trust has never been misplaced. Such faith has never been denied.

XIII

THE ETERNAL SEARCH

Every man's search is after God because everyone is searching for something that will make him whole. But everyone does not know, or quite realize, that he really is searching after God. We have separated religion from everyday life; we have tried to separate Life from living, and God from nature. God means that invisible Presence in the universe, that Divine Power which animates everything, and that Law of Mind which controls everything. But we have come to feel that the kingdom of God is not really at hand, that it is to transpire in a dim and unknown future.

This was not the attitude Jesus took when he proclaimed that the kingdom really is at hand; when he told us that if we would find God in ourselves and in each other and in nature, we would find happiness and completion. We would find what the human heart not only longs for but absolutely needs, particularly in these times of stress and strain when the question arises from countless thousands: What is it all about? Why this confusion and uncertainty and fear and doubt?

I believe that out of this great confusion will come an equally great certainty, and out of all this doubt will grow a faith. It surely will if enough people turn to that Divine Source from which everything springs. God really is the object of our search since Divine Power alone can make us whole.

So now, as never before in human history, we need God. We need to enter into a close communion with the living Spirit and feel the warm embrace of Its eternal Presence around us. We need to know that we are not pawns on a checkerboard of chance, that there is a real and deep meaning to existence — a meaning that includes this life and everything in it, and after this a life to which we may look forward with happy anticipation. Nothing less than this can give us happiness and peace.

Perhaps at first thought it may seem a selfish desire to say we want this and we want that and we want something else. Yet it is impossible for us to think of anything as being entirely separate from ourselves. We cannot think of Life without thinking of Its connection and relationship to the self. We cannot think of others without thinking of their relationship to us.

The singer wishes to sing; the dancer wishes to dance; the man engaged in business wishes to be a success; the man with a family wishes to provide for them and be happy with them. Self-expression is not selfishness. Selfishness is in seeking our individual good at the expense of others. Self-expression means that we live with others in happiness, giving to each the privilege of expressing every talent he possesses and rejoicing with him in his success.

There is nothing wrong with self-expression. Life has entered into each of us in an individual way, animating everything we do and apparently always urging us to greater things, as though there were no limit to the expansion of the individual life. But we are so constituted that the greatest self-expression includes our relationship with others and our relationship with everything in life.

Jesus told us that if we find God we will find all these things, for all these things are added to the great discovery. Jesus made heaven and earth come together. He did not say that there is a heaven which God has provided for us in a life after this life; he said that heaven is present with us. Did he not say to the one who died with him: "To day shalt thou be with me in paradise"? Jesus said that the kingdom of God is at hand and that everyone who comes into this kingdom, through finding a right relationship with God, will find love, friendship, success, and happiness, here and now. Jesus never condemned the personal desire we all have to live happily and successfully.

The search after God is not the search for some abstract principle or some future state of being. Our search is to find that Something right where we are, to discover that Something in each other and in nature. The Psalmist said that the earth is filled with the glory of God, and we all know that the great teaching of Mahatma Gandhi was not that we should renounce the world but that we should find God in the world. It is this finding of God in everything we do and in every person and every thing we contact that is our real search.

The interesting thing we discover when we read history is that the great examples of the human race have been those who have found Something that can give us the assurance that all is well, that back of the fear and doubt and uncertainty of life there is a great Assurance, that at the center of the storm there is a place of Peace, at the center of every person we can find God. The search is both an individual and a collective one. But, as always, we must start with the individual, and that individual means you, and it means me.

Have you and I actually and persistently tried to find God in each other? I am afraid we have not. Well, there is no use blaming ourselves. It does one no good to beat his breast and exclaim how unworthy he is. This merely adds more confusion to an already disturbed mind. The searcher after God must learn to forgive himself and everyone else, to forget even his own weaknesses as he seeks strength. The searcher after peace must forget his confusion and meditate on peace, and as he does this he discovers that the confusion disappears. The searcher after God may be sure of this — he will have to find God in himself before he can discover God in others. This is why Jesus said that the blind cannot lead the blind; there must be a seeing eye.

When John the Baptist was asked, "What shall I do to avoid the wrath to come?" he answered something after this manner: My friend, I have not come to tell you how to avoid some future wrath that is to be visited on you. I have come proclaiming that the kingdom of God is already at hand.

This is the attitude we should take, that Life holds nothing against us; It desires only our good; It wants us to be well, happy, and successful, only It wants us to play the game of life the way it is supposed to be played — in unity and cooperation with others.

These are the only rules that Life has laid down for us. It has not demanded that we do something that is impossible. It has not told us that we have to understand something that only a few great intellects can comprehend. It has not even told us that we all have to become saints before we can enter into the kingdom of heaven. It has merely said this: Here I am. I am Truth; I am Wisdom; I am Love; I am Peace; and I am eternal Goodness. Accept me!

Suppose, then, you and I start all over, beginning right now, and let us see if we cannot learn to forget all the heartache and sorrow and pain, all the fear, frustration and uncertainty, and go back inside ourselves until we find that little child who is not afraid because, by some Divine instinct within him, he knows that "underneath are the everlasting arms."

Are we afraid of becoming that spontaneous child again lest someone think we are foolish? Well, who is there among us who would not again be happy as a child? Who is there among us who would not recapture the dream of youth? No, if the greatest man who ever lived has told us that we must become as little children, we need not be afraid of becoming childlike.

Remember, childlike does not imply being childish, silly, or foolish. Rather, it implies the attitude a scientist must have as he stands in awe before the majesty and might of the laws of nature. It is the wonder that a great mathematician must have as he contemplates the infinity of numbers. It is the reaching out toward the essence of beauty which every great artist feels when he captures the glory of a sunset or the soft, radiant pathway of the moon across the water. We need not be afraid of being childlike. Rather, we should fear not to be childlike, for only through an attitude of faith and trust in the Universe can we ever hope to recapture our lost paradise.

If our search for God happily results in our finding Him, everyone around us will soon discover this fact. If our search for happiness makes us happy without robbing others, everyone we contact will be exposed to this happiness — it will become contagious. If our search is for love and we find it, we shall become lovable and those around us will love us because we have first loved them. If our search for security finally leads us to the place where we are no longer afraid, everyone who contacts us will be lifted up because of our faith; they will be strengthened because of our strength, and they will feel secure in our security.

So let us try to find God in ourselves and in each other, and not be afraid to look for Him in human events. And just as surely as we do this, we shall find Him. "Ask, and it shall be given you; seek, and ye shall find; knock, and it shall be opened unto you."